Finding One's Way

Finding One's Way

How Mentoring Can Lead to Dynamic Leadership

Gary M. Crow
L. Joseph Matthews

CORWIN PRESS, INC.
A Sage Publications Company
Thousand Oaks, California

For information:

Corwin Press, Inc.
A Sage Publications Company
2455 Teller Road
Thousand Oaks, California 91320
E-mail: order@corwin.sagepub.com

SAGE Publications Ltd.
6 Bonhill Street
London EC2A 4PU
United Kingdom

SAGE Publications India Pvt. Ltd.
M-32 Market
Greater Kailash I
New Delhi 110 048 India

Printed in the United States of America

Library of Congress Cataloging-in-Publication Data

Crow, Gary Monroe, 1947-
    Finding one's way: How mentoring can lead to dynamic leadership
    / by Gary M. Crow, L. Joseph Matthews.
       p. cm.
    Includes bibliographical references and index.
    ISBN 0-8039-6545-1 (acid-free paper). — ISBN 0-8039-6546-X (pbk.:
acid-free paper)
    1. Mentoring in education—United States. 2. School principals—
Training of—United States. 3. Educational leadership—United
States. I. Matthews, L. Joseph, 1950- . II. Title.
LB1731.4.C76 1997
371.2'012—dc21   97-21094

This book is printed on acid-free paper.

98 99 00 01 02 10 9 8 7 6 5 4 3 2 1

Editorial Assistant: Kristen L. Gibson
Production Editor: Sanford Robinson
Production Assistant: Denise Santoyo
Typesetter: Rebecca Evans
Indexer: Teri Greenberg
Cover Designer: Marcia M. Rosenburg

Contents

Preface

From Homer's *Odyssey* and Moses' travels in the wilderness to the Native American "spirit-guide," cultures have used "journeys" to prepare their leaders for change. New role changes resulting from school reform agendas such as site-based management, school choice, and collaboration present an urgent need for unique journeys for school administrators. Administrators at all career stages—intern, new, and mid-career—need professional development strategies to help them "find their way" in the journeys they must take.

A primary way to help administrators on these journeys involves arrangements by universities and school districts, either individually or in partnership, to identify veteran principals to serve as partners—mentors. These mentors help prospective, new, and veteran administrators develop the necessary knowledge, skills, behaviors, and values to be dynamic leaders.

Why We Wrote This Book

Discussions of mentoring tend to occur in a theoretical vacuum, ignoring the conceptual foundations that both justify and organize mentoring. The literature on occupational socialization throughout the career provides a valuable way to understand the power of the mentoring experience and to focus attention on how mentoring can produce dynamic school leaders.

In addition to the lack of a theoretical understanding of mentoring, the practice of mentoring is typically unintended and unsupported. Mentors are often selected without a great deal of thought and rarely trained. Mentoring arrangements are frequently established only for prospective or new principals. Yet, administrators at all career stages, especially in times of reform, are on a professional leadership journey that can benefit from mentoring that is planned, supported, and evaluated. Leaving the mentoring and socializing of school principals to chance counters the professional ethic of education. Schools are replete with principals who have emerged through survival as the fittest. In this book, we suggest a different approach, in which the norm is leaders mentoring other leaders throughout their administrative careers.

Our interest in mentoring intensified with our previous work, which culminated in a book, *Leadership: A Relevant and Realistic Role for Principals* (Crow, Matthews, & McCleary, 1996). As we studied principal preparation programs and the existing literature on administrative socialization, the importance of mentoring became paramount. We found that principals identified their primary source of help in becoming a school leader as other school leaders. Our research in Utah and in two other states helped us understand the overt and subtle ways principal interns are socialized by veteran administrators. We also discovered not only that mentoring occurs when the principal is a student or a neophyte but that mentoring and socialization are evident in veteran administrators' careers. We determined that since mentors guide and develop both experienced and inexperienced leaders, examination of the mentoring phenomenon could provide important insight into the socialization process of administrators and their continued development in school leadership.

Our approach to mentoring in this book is based on our understanding of the socialization and mentoring literature and our belief that socialization, and therefore mentoring, should be a career-long experience. We use literature, our own research, and our own experiences to develop an understanding of mentoring across the career. We begin the book by introducing the concept of mentoring (Chapter 1) and a model of socialization, which forms the context in which mentoring occurs (Chapter 2). We then describe the socialization and mentoring processes of aspiring school principals, especially those who are involved in principal internships (Chapters 3 and 4). The assistant principalship has undergone considerable change since the late 1980s, and the socialization and mentoring of this group of administrators deserves attention (Chapter 5). We also believe new principals, especially those in schools seeking to reform, have special socialization and mentoring needs (Chapters 6 and 7). Many educators and citizens believe that veteran principals and assistant principals have "arrived." We believe otherwise. In fact, mid-career administrators need the assistance and companionship that mentors can provide. If school reform is to be realized, mid-career administrators must be convinced to change their practice and values. Thus, socialization and mentoring of mid-career administrators are critical issues (Chapters 8 and 9). The mentoring process we propose is not a casual, informal, "get a mentor as you can" approach. Universities and school districts need to develop formal mentoring programs. We provide an outline of the major issues of planning, mentor selection, matching, training, and evaluation necessary for such formal programs (Chapter 10). We also identify the unique ingredients in establishing these mentoring programs for administrators at different stages of the administrative journey.

The Audience for This Book

We wrote this book for those who are mentors, those who want to be mentors, those who want to have mentors, and those who are involved in developing mentor programs:

- School leaders, especially principals and assistant principals, who want to develop as dynamic leaders and help others become leaders to make our schools more dynamic environments for children and adults
- District office administrators, directors, and coordinators who establish professional development programs for new assistant principals, new principals, and veteran administrators
- Regional and state administrators, directors, and coordinators who develop leadership academies, programs, activities, and conferences for school administrators
- Professors, directors, and instructors in university preparation programs who help prepare and instruct aspiring principals, direct and supervise principal internships, and instruct and develop mid-career school leaders in advanced programs

Acknowledgments

As with socialization and mentoring, the influences on this book are multiple and intense. Several groups of individuals have inspired, supported, informed, and prodded us in this endeavor. First, our students contributed not only illustrations but the inspiration for helping mentors provide more effective experiences for interns and other administrators. Their willingness to be interviewed, to complete surveys, to listen to our ideas, and to spontaneously report their experiences have been essential elements for developing our understanding of mentoring and socialization processes.

Gracia A. Alkema, of Corwin Press, was an immense help in clarifying our ideas about mentoring and developing a way to say what we wanted to say so others would understand. Her encouragement was critical to the initiation of this project. We appreciate her support and the technical assistance of the Corwin editorial staff.

Our colleagues at the University of Utah, Department of Educational Administration, were, as always, highly supportive and encouraging throughout this project. They contributed to this book with their expertise and encouragement and they provided an environment that made the difficult moments more bearable. Two graduate assistants were especially helpful in this project. Rebecca Raybould spent countless hours securing bibliographic sources and documenting them for the reference list. Also, her valuable comments contributed to several chapters. At the end of the process, Kevin Walthers's proofreading helped ensure that our manuscript made sense. We appreciate their skills and contributions.

Families are an important part of not only our personal but our professional lives. Sue, David, and Jimmy Matthews; and Judy, Amy, and Laura Crow patiently supported and encouraged us throughout this process. If family members can mentor, they mentored us in countless and loving ways.

Both of us throughout our lives have had the opportunity to be influenced by several mentors. Some have taught us valuable lessons regarding our jobs, others have sponsored us in our careers, and still others have supported us through personally troubling times. Del Wasden, Merrell Hansen, Ivan Muse, David Sperry, Dan Lortie, Nona Weekes, Katherine O'Donnell, Lavonn Brown, and Don Wester have been special mentors for us. This book would not have been possible without the personal experiences that we had with these women and men. To them, we say, "Thank you for the incredible gift of mentoring us."

GARY M. CROW AND L. JOSEPH MATTHEWS
Salt Lake City, Utah

About the Authors

Gary M. Crow is Associate Professor of Educational Administration at The University of Utah. He holds a PhD degree from The University of Chicago. He has conducted research in several urban areas, focusing on the school principalship and the socialization of principals at both entry and mid-career stages. He has written numerous journal articles on leadership, the principalship, socialization, and school restructuring and recently coauthored a book, *Leadership: A Relevant and Realistic Role for Principals,* with L. Joseph Matthews and Lloyd McCleary. He has served in various administrative positions in preschool and alternative school settings.

L. Joseph Matthews is Clinical Professor of Educational Administration at The University of Utah. He holds an EdD degree from Brigham Young University. He teaches courses in the school principalship, supervises administrative interns, and has developed and implemented a training program for mentor principals. He is currently president of the Utah Consortium for Educational Administration and has served as president of the Utah Secondary School Principal Association and director of the Utah Principals Academy. His work has appeared in national and regional publications as well as the book *Leadership: A Relevant and Realistic Role for Principals,* coauthored with Gary M. Crow and Lloyd McCleary. He has served as a junior and senior high school principal.

1

Finding One's Way— Alone or With Others

The journey is a common metaphor, perhaps the most common, to represent our heroic and not so heroic life passages. The journey appeals to us because it helps us make sense of our past, present, and future as well as the process of learning how to live, work, and play. Although often depicted as lonely passages through difficult circumstances, journeys are also made with others. The administrative journey, which is focus of this book, can be taken alone or with others.

In this chapter, we introduce the concept of mentoring as a learning tool for the administrative journey. After an introductory discussion of the meaning of mentoring, we turn our attention to the people, purposes, pitfalls and benefits, functions, content, and methods of mentoring. Discussion of these general topics will paint the broad strokes of a model of mentoring that we reinforce and expand in the next chapter, on socialization.

The Meaning of Mentoring

To understand mentoring, we begin with its history. The source of the term *mentor* is found in Homer's epic *The Odyssey*. When Odysseus left on an adventurous journey to fight in the Trojan War, he gave the responsibility of nurturing his son, Telemachus, to his loyal friend, Mentor. In Odysseus's absence, Mentor educated and guided Telemachus. This education included every facet of his life, that is, physical, intellectual, spiritual, social, and administrative development (Clawson, 1980). Mentor not only provided help and assistance to Telemachus, but what is most important, he taught Telemachus to think and act for himself (Kay, 1990).

Homer gave us the name *Mentor*, which commonly refers to someone with more experience who teaches someone with less experience. This aspect of mentoring has also led to the word *protégé*, from the French term *protegere*, meaning one who is protected by a person with experience and influence. With the passage of time, however, and with the demands of differing situations, the typical Mentor-Telemachus model, or mentor-protégé relationship, has changed considerably.

The 20-year relationship between Mentor and Telemachus can seldom be duplicated on our administrative journey. We use the term mentor in a broader, more dynamic and metaphorical manner. Our definition of a mentor in an administrative context involves a person who is active, dynamic, visionary, knowledgeable, and skilled; who has a committed philosophy that keeps the teaching and learning of students in focus; and who guides other leaders to be similarly active and dynamic. The process of mentoring dynamic school leaders involves more than a single mentor, more than a single setting, and more than just "rookie protégés."

Perhaps we can clarify our understanding of mentoring by attending to what it is not. Altounyan (1995) proposed an image of what mentoring is not by using another Greek myth. Procrustes, who lived in a cave, often invited visitors to extravagant banquets. At the end of the evening, Procrustes invited his tired visitors to stay the night. If the visitors were too short for the bed, Procrustes put them on racks to stretch them until they fitted better. If they were too long, Procrustes chopped off the bits dangling over the end of the bed.

Altounyan (1995) applied this image to two aspects of mentoring. First, mentoring offers a rich banquet of many different aspects of life and work. Second, mentoring is not cutting people down to the size the mentor prefers or the organization requires. "Mentoring is too rich and individual for that: it is not a Procrustean bed" (Altounyan, 1995, p. 29).

A mentor, likewise, is not only a teacher or coach who focuses primarily on the task and the results. Mentors focus on individuals and their development. They act as confidants willing to play the part of an adversary if needed, to listen and to question so protégés can broaden their own view.

Megginson and Clutterbuck (1995) illustrated this concept by elaborating on Homer's representation of Mentor as an earthly form taken by the goddess Athene. When Odysseus returns from his wandering and he and his son Telemachus are faced with their final challenge, Athene, the mentor, does not use all her powers to give them victory but continues to put the strength and courage of both Odysseus and Telemachus on trial. Athene withdraws, taking the shape of a swallow to perch on the smoky beam of the hall. "The power of this image is that it puts mentors where they need to be, out of the action, looking on and encouraging, rather than taking over and doing the work for the learner" (Megginson & Clutterbuck, 1995, p. 28).

The People of Mentoring: Travelers, Guides, and Passengers

Mentoring on the administrative journey involves three kinds of individuals: travelers, guides, and passengers. Travelers are those wanting and needing assistance. Guides are mentors for the travelers. Passengers are those on the journey who also benefit from the mentoring process. They may be university faculty, district administrators, teachers and students in the school, and family and friends. In this section, we discuss these roles in the mentoring process.

Travelers

Much as we prepare for, begin, and continue on a journey, principals travel through career stages. This book is organized around four career stages in which principals advance in their careers:

1. Principal Interns: Aspiring principals who are currently in university preparation programs, studying school leadership as a career and leaving teaching to join administrative ranks

2. New Assistant Principals: Individuals who are entering their first administrative jobs, usually coming directly from the classroom or from another nonadministrative role such as counseling

3. New Principals: Individuals who have been assistant principals for several years and now have become principals or who are entering a principalship directly

4. Mid-career principals and assistant principals: Veterans who have been in administration for several years

As we discuss in subsequent chapters, these stages are characterized by different needs, which influence different content and methods of mentoring.

Guides

In our journey metaphor, we suggest that mentors act as guides, but within that function they can and do take on other roles. Odell (1990) identified these different roles that mentors play, for example, trusted guide (Homer), teacher (Levinson, Darrow, Klein, Levinson, & McKee, 1978), sponsor (Schein, 1978), challenger (Daloz, 1983), and confidant (Gehrke & Kay, 1984). We refer to these roles in subsequent chapters as we discuss the mentoring functions at the four career stages.

We distinguish two types of mentors, primary and secondary (Phillips-Jones, 1982). Primary mentors provide a wide scope of assistance and in-depth mentoring. They mentor the protégé in professional, career, and personal matters in and outside the professional role. For example, a primary mentor working with a new assistant principal may go golfing with this protégé for recreation, relaxation, and companionship. While golfing, they may engage in discussions of professional skills or problems as well as personal adjustments necessary for the new assistant principal.

Secondary mentors provide a more limited scope and degree of mentoring. Common concerns for secondary mentors are helping protégés in technical skills, knowledge, or processes. As an example, a new elementary principal may have a primary mentor who guides and assists him or her in learning how to act in the new school, district, and profession, but the new principal may have to rely on a secondary mentor for particular assistance in learning the district's supervision and evaluation policy. This secondary mentor can teach and advise the new principal about the policy and continue to monitor the new principal's understanding of it. Their relationship is important and may develop into a friendship, but it does not have the same significance or scope as that with a primary mentor.

We suggest that principals rely more on primary mentors in early career stages and less as the principals mature. Principals often hold primary mentors in high regard, thinking of these persons as the ones who gave them the start they needed in each career stage. The relationship between primary mentors and protégés may not last a lifetime, but the respect and admiration will. Secondary mentors can be involved with principals in each career stage, but they often come and go as needed. The number of mentors, especially secondary mentors, usually increases as the principal matures in the profession. We call this concept networking and we discuss it further in subsequent chapters.

Soon after the aspiring principal embarks on the journey, peer relationships usually develop. Peer mentors are colleagues who take on primary or secondary mentor roles with each other. Peer mentors, who can be present at all four career stages, share problems, strategies, professional and personal information, friendship, and support. Examples include principal interns with peer mentors in university cohorts or classes, assistant principals with other assistant principals, and new and mid-career principals with each other as peer mentors. Principals in all career stages tend to find isolation in their profession if they do not seek out and use peer mentors.

Passengers

Journeys also may include passengers who join the traveler for part of the way. These passengers are deeply involved with the journey and may have personal interests and investment but are not in the role of either guide or traveler. These individuals are involved indirectly in the mentoring process. Passengers include university faculty, district administrators, teachers, students, family, and friends. The following examples illustrate how passengers can be involved in the mentoring process:

- University faculty view the internship experience as a critical period in which interns learn to apply theory to practice. Many university programs appoint mentors to adjunct faculty positions because of their important role in the development of principal interns.

- District administrators are interested in the development and success of principals in all four career stages. They help in establishing internship placement opportunities and sponsor mentor programs for new assistant principals and principals. They are also involved in the continued development and improvement of veteran principals.

- Teachers and students are interested in the mentoring process of principals because it affects them directly. They see the results of the mentoring process in the teaching and learning that dynamic leadership influences. As we describe in later chapters, teachers and students play a significant role in the socialization of school principals. In some circumstances, teachers may act as mentors to administrators.

- Family and friends also are involved in the mentoring process. Both groups need to give support to the principal in role identification and role changes. The principal's relationships with family and friends are affected during particular periods of the administrative journey.

The Goal of Mentoring: The Journey's Destinations

The administrative journey includes a series of destinations that we can describe as goals of the journey. Arriving at a scenic overlook is a rewarding experience, after which travelers press on toward still better scenic spots.

To understand the primary goal of mentoring, we must first take a short trip to the museum to understand our past. Rooted in U.S. educational heritage is the term *principal.* The word originated from the term *principal teacher,* which in the 19th century was used synonymously with *head teacher* or *headmaster.* As the 20th century emerged and schools grew from one-teacher systems to multi-teacher systems, a teacher, often the one with the most experience, was designated to be a director of the school. This *principal-teacher* was given the responsibility of helping other teachers, especially the new recruits who aspired to be pedagogues. These young masters and marms came to the school with some general education but often with little teaching preparation. They usually learned teaching methods from those who were teaching, especially the principal-teacher. "The men and women who managed schools during that era have been described as teachers of teachers" (Beck & Murphy, 1993, p. 193).

From a more contemporary view, Barth (1990) contended that principals should view teachers, students, and parents as colleagues, partners, colearners, and friends. He argued that principals working with others in the system can create a "community of learners." We propose that a major goal of mentoring is to establish a community of learners in which principals themselves are learners and instill learning in others.

We also can identify a goal of mentoring as the kind of principal being developed. We use the term *dynamic* as an adjective to describe the kind of principal leadership that schools need today. We suggest that leadership be that energetic style described by Goldring and Rallis (1993):

> A school that is truly changing needs a principal who can articulate a vision, provide direction, facilitate those who are working for the change, coordinate the different groups, and balance the various forces impacting schools today. . . . While much of what they do is similar to the work of a traditional principal, principals-in-charge approach their work differently. First, they recognize the forces that impact schools and education today, and second, they use these forces as resources rather than hindrances or burdens. (p. 133)

The primary goal of mentoring should be to develop dynamic school leaders who cultivate a learning community for other leaders, teachers, staff members, parents, and students. In subsequent chapters, we return to this major goal as well as identify other goals of mentoring unique to individual career stages.

"Lions and Tigers and Bears, Oh My!" Understanding the Pitfalls and Benefits of Mentoring

Dorothy's journey in Oz led her through many dangers. Her quest to find the Wizard and return to Kansas was important to her and kept her traveling on her journey. The new friends she made along the way helped her through these dangers until she reached her destinations. Although mentoring can have important goals, it has pitfalls:

- Mentors may have personal agendas to fulfill and therefore may not always have the best interests of others in mind (Muse, Wasden, & Thomas, 1988). Because of selfish concerns or ulterior motives, some mentors may want the prestige, honor, or status that may come from mentoring.

- Mentoring relationships may become too protective and controlling (Daresh & Playko, 1993). Mentoring may cause emotional attachments that distort accurate assessment of potential and limitations. Likewise, mentors may be puppeteers who limit the protégé's development.

- Mentoring may restrict problem-solving and decision-making perspectives. A mentor may be so committed to a particular style of leadership that other possible approaches are not considered.

- Mentors may be considered experts or dunces in all fields. Being in a mentoring relationship may support a polarized belief that mentors have either all the right answers or no answers. In reality, all mentors have strengths and weaknesses.

- A mentoring relationship may create dependency. Instead of developing an interdependent relationship, protégés may cultivate such reliance on the mentor that reasonable decisions cannot be made without consultation with the mentor.

- Mentors can encourage cloning (Hay, 1995). In a review of research on leader succession and socialization, Hart (1991, 1993) contended that mentors can constrain innovation and that using only established veterans as mentors virtually guarantees the reproduction of existing roles.

Benefits of the Mentoring Process

We would seldom travel if all we found were pitfalls. In this section, we identify the benefits for each of the three roles in the mentoring process: the mentor (guide), the protégé (traveler), and the passengers.

Mentor Benefits. Benefits for the mentor may be implied, but they are highly meaningful. Being a mentor strengthens the leader in the following ways:

- Mentors gain a renewed enthusiasm for the profession (Daresh & Playko, 1993). The relationship helps mentors avoid isolation, renew their own growth, and collaborate on dynamic leadership and educational innovation.
- Mentors gain new insights. Megginson and Clutterbuck (1995) reported that many mentors learned computer and technical skills through their relationship with protégés. Through collaborative and reflective discussions, mentors expand their understanding of leadership.
- Mentors gain the opportunity to evaluate critically their intuitive processes. When mentors articulate what they do, how they do it, and why they do it, the process allows them to reflect on their own leadership processes and styles in a unique way (Megginson & Clutterbuck, 1995).
- Mentors gain the satisfaction of being a teacher again. Indeed, many principals express frustration at being separated from the teaching process when they move into administration. Mentors regain the interaction and satisfaction of teaching when they establish mentoring relationships (Daresh & Playko, 1990).
- Mentors gain a network for ideas and opportunities for promotion. Working in a mentoring relationship opens doors that were not previously available. Not only are more ideas generated, but career opportunities increase as well (Daresh & Playko, 1993).
- Mentors gain validation of their importance and the importance of their work. From school, district, or university personnel, mentors receive accolades for mentoring. In a role for

which few tributes are given, this endorsement can be meaningful to principals (Daresh & Playko, 1993).

- Mentors gain long-lasting and meaningful friendships. The associations that develop often continue in formal or informal relationships long after the formal mentoring process has concluded. These friendships emerge as valuable assets for principals in later years (Roche, 1979).

From our experience in working with mentors and principal interns, another predominant theme emerged. Mentors, after having worked with an intern, requested another intern. Consistently, we have found that the mentors enjoy the experience and miss it when it is absent.

Protégé Benefits. Benefits for protégés may seem obvious, such as developing greater insight into self, learning the tricks of the trade, and packing a bag full of tips. We have found, however, more subtle gains:

- *Exposure to new ideas and creativity.* When protégés encounter different experiences, new ideas for practice emerge. They become more creative, although most creativity involves adapting ideas from others. Torrance (1984) found that people who had mentors were more creatively productive.
- *Visibility with key personnel.* Visibility with others may influence the fate of protégés, especially for future career opportunities. As acquaintances are made with others in the profession, visibility opportunities increase.
- *Protection from damaging situations.* Mentors often shield protégés from untimely or potentially damaging contact with certain situations that the protégé may not be ready to address. One of the mentor's key responsibilities is to outline harms that loom ahead. If protégés become too visible too soon and make mistakes, they may limit future career opportunities. This does not mean, however, that the mentor should shelter the protégé so that growth and socialization are delayed.
- *Opportunities for challenging and risk-taking activities.* The mentor's support can be critical for the protégé to face challenging

situations and to proceed with risk-taking ventures. This is especially important for administrative interns and new principals for whom challenging opportunities may seem too threatening to venture upon on their own. Interns and new principals need to be challenged and coached to continue, even if mistakes occur. Mentors often shield the intern from the harmful effects of making wrong decisions, yet the protégé learns from the experience to handle similar future situations.

- *Increased confidence and competence.* Even when protégés make mistakes, mentors find ways to support the protégés and praise the things they do well, while helping them understand what could be done better the next time.
- *Improved reflection.* Working with mentors allows protégés to reflect more on their practices. As they talk with mentors, they become more insightful about their actions. Kanter (1977) suggested that individuals gain "reflective power" from their mentors.

Passenger Benefits. As we previously suggested, passengers such as university faculty, district administrators, teachers, students, family, and friends are involved in the administrative journey. The mentoring process is also beneficial to these individuals:

- Administrators with mentoring programs in their districts have more capable leaders. Daresh and Playko (1993) found that leaders in the school districts with mentoring programs tended to be more energized by the mentoring process.
- A community of learners becomes more apparent. An attitude of lifelong learning is created among those who are involved in mentoring programs (Daresh & Playko, 1993).
- District administrators gain better recruits and candidates for administrative positions. Visibility and exposure allow more individuals to emerge as successful candidates for administrative positions (Nash & Treffinger, 1993).
- University faculty have a means to link theory and practice. Associations between internship experiences and course subject matter occur more frequently than when no internship is in place.

- Teachers and students gain the opportunity to work with more dynamic leaders. Principals who are involved with others in collegial and reflective mentoring are more collaborative and interested in improving teaching and learning.
- Family and friends benefit from protégés learning to balance multiple roles. Through mentoring, protégés tend to have a clearer perception of the roles they play with school, family, and friends.

The Functions of Mentoring

In her studies of mentors in the corporate world, Kram (1985) suggested two functions of mentoring. The first is the career function, which is focused on learning the ropes and preparing for a career move. The second is the psychosocial function, which involves the development of the individual in his or her social environment. Whereas career functions serve primarily to aid career advancement, psychosocial functions affect the individual on a personal level, clarifying role identity.

Kram's (1985) career function included both professional and career issues of mentoring. We, however, distinguish professional development from career development. Career functions in school leadership are quite different from those in most other professions. Few upper-level school administrator positions are available for advancement. Sponsoring a protégé is a different mentoring activity for school leaders from what it is for corporate managers. Because of the ever-changing, dynamic nature of school leadership, the professional development needs of school principals are different from career development needs. Our mentoring model therefore incorporates three functions. The professional development function is focused on the development of knowledge, skills, behaviors, and values for dynamic school leadership. The career development function of mentoring is focused on career satisfaction, career awareness, and career advancement. The psychosocial development function involves personal and emotional well-being, as well as role expectation, clarification, and conflict.

The Content of Mentoring: Traveling Tips

On some journeys, a guide begins the adventure with an orientation offering traveling tips: knowledge about what we need to expect, skills about how to travel safely and effectively, and behaviors and values about how to handle situations. After the orientation, the guide continues to train, teach, and coach. Travelers learn the knowledge, skills, behaviors, and values for a successful journey. We consider this information as the content of mentoring and the curriculum for learning dynamic leadership. Content has long been a topic of debate, since not everyone agrees on what principals need to learn.

Content has both technical and cultural aspects (Greenfield, 1985c). Technical aspects include learning "how things are done," that is, the instrumental knowledge and skills necessary to perform the job. Cultural aspects include learning "how things are done around here," that is, the expressive norms, values, and beliefs of a school culture. Learning the technical "how to" but not the "how to around here" can be detrimental for principals if they move from one setting to another setting or from one career stage to another career stage. We discuss these aspects of content in Chapter 2 and subsequent chapters as they pertain to each career stage.

We suggest that in determining the content needed in the mentoring process, the mentor and protégé reflect on the protégé's needs, especially those needs in four areas: knowledge, skills, behaviors, and values. Knowledge content involves theoretical, community, and personal information. Interpersonal relationships, communication, and supervision are examples of skill content. Content related to behavior includes teacher selection, networking, and discipline. Value content includes cultural and professional norms, beliefs, and assumptions. The three functions of mentoring—professional, career, and psychosocial development—include content from each of these four areas.

The Methods of Mentoring: Learning to Drive

The guide can tell the travelers the way to go and wish them well, or the guide can accompany the travelers, helping them learn

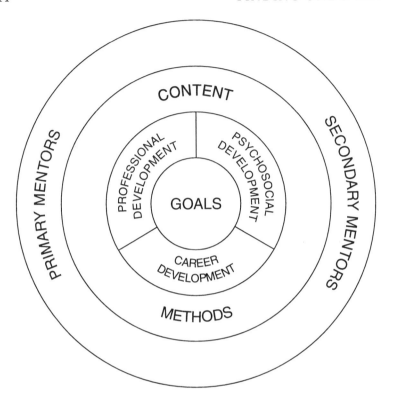

Figure 1.1. Functions, Content, and Methods of Mentoring

to guide themselves. In this manner, the guide delicately balances taking over and sitting back and watching. What the guide does or allows the traveler to do is what we term the methods of mentoring.

Methods in the mentoring process include the ways the mentor helps guide the protégé in professional, career, and psychosocial development. The methods chosen by the mentor and the protégé depend on the setting, the career stage of the protégé, and the personalities of the mentor and protégé. We suggest a reflective conference to assess and analyze the best methods to employ. We treat methods in more detail in subsequent chapters that deal with each career stage.

A Look Back and a Look Ahead

Traveling on a journey always involves looking back and looking ahead. Likewise, in this book, we will keep the reader in touch with what we have discussed and what we are about to discuss.

In this chapter, we laid the groundwork for our understanding of the meaning of mentoring, the people involved in the mentoring process, the purpose of mentoring, and some benefits and pitfalls. We also identified the functions, content, and methods of mentoring. Figure 1.1 illustrates the relationships among these elements. The goal(s) of mentoring are at the core and guide the rest of the mentoring process. Each of the three functions of mentoring—professional, career, and psychosocial—is guided by this purpose. Finally, the content and methods of mentoring depend on the three functions. This model rests in a larger context that includes career stage and organizational setting. This model guides our discussion of mentoring at the four career stages: intern, new assistant principal, new principal, and mid-career administrator.

Ahead, we place mentoring in the broad context of socialization. Much as a driver places the destination and routes of a trip within the larger region and uses a map to guide the subsequent travel, the next chapter provides the map for the administrative journey in which mentoring is a vehicle.

2

Mapping the Journey

Socialization as the Context of Mentoring

In the previous chapter, we used the metaphor of the journey as a way to understand mentoring and the goal of developing dynamic school leaders. In this chapter, we generate the map for this journey. We use the idea of a map to describe what happens to individuals as they experience mentoring and to understand the context of mentoring.

We typically use maps to direct a journey—to get from a starting point to a destination, to keep from getting lost, and to rescue ourselves if we get lost. This, of course, assumes we are strangers and have not traveled this region before or for a long time. We find our destination on the map and usually follow the shortest route—assuming time is the primary criterion for our journey. Occasionally, we choose an alternate scenic route if some other criterion is primary.

Another form of mapping is rarely used except by scouts and cartographers. Maps can be something we create rather than something we follow. These maps become critical if no one has previously traveled this area, if no former traveler has created a map for us to follow, or if the only available maps do not include sufficient detail to make for an efficient and successful trip. On our first journey as strangers in a new land, we can draw a map to ease our next journey or help others who come after us.

When new administrators take on their first assignments, they use maps that others have created for them—other administrators, teachers, parents, or even students. They also are strangers in a new land. These maps seldom have sufficient detail to enable these administrators to progress on their journey or reach their destinations. Thus, they must develop their own maps of where they are, where they have been, and where they are going. In this book, we contend that interns, assistant principals, new principals, and even mid-career administrators are both following others' maps and actively generating their own maps. Mentoring, if successful, provides a map and the support for creating a new map for this administrative journey.

In this chapter, we use socialization theory and research to develop a framework—our map—for understanding the context of mentoring. The mentoring literature has typically developed in a theoretical and, in some cases, empirical vacuum. Atheoretical treatments of mentoring ignore both the rationale for mentoring and the context of the individual's career, within which mentoring occurs. Examining mentoring in the theoretical framework of socialization clarifies the goals of mentoring and guides the choice of mentoring content and methods to achieve these goals. Understanding mentoring as a socialization method allows us to see its inherent qualities in context, that is, the nature of mentoring that aids professional learning throughout the career. Without a theoretical framework in mind, we run the risk of once again throwing another trick into the professional development hopper with little hope that we will come out with more dynamic school leaders.

The classic definition of socialization is Brim's (1966): "the processes by which persons acquire the knowledge, skills, and dispositions that make them more or less able members of their society" (p. 3). Mentoring is a socialization strategy to help individuals acquire the knowledge, skills, behaviors, and values necessary to perform the role of school administrator. Since mentoring is not the only method used in administrator socialization, its properties and goals are likely affected by other methods. For example, at the principal intern stage, when mentoring is used simultaneously with university graduate education, the two socialization forms either complement or contradict each other depending on how they are organized and coordinated (Schein, 1968/1988).

The Basis for the Map:
Socialization Literature

We do not attempt in this section to provide an exhaustive literature review but to contribute a useful outline of the major concepts and issues of socialization theory and research that inform mentoring. The section includes literature on the characteristics, stages, methods, and outcomes of socialization. Along the way, we critique this literature.

Characteristics of Socialization

"Socialization" in our common language is fraught with negative meaning:

> To American ears, attuned by Constitution and conviction to the full expression of individuality, socialization tends to sound alien and vaguely sinister. Some equate it with the propagation of socialism, but even when it is correctly understood as the development of social conformity, the prospect makes most of us cringe. (Pascale, 1984, p. 28)

In this first section, we redefine socialization in a broader (and we hope less conformist) way than its typical use.

Like maps, socialization has numerous features that more or less help in finding our way. Maps have perspective. For example, we notice the difference between a flat road map and a topographical map. Maps also vary in their content, for example, whether or not they include rivers, state boundaries, and landmarks. Moreover, maps differ depending on context, as, for example, state maps versus a globe. In this section, we discuss perspective, content, and context as three major socialization characteristics.

Perspectives.

Socialization, at any age, is a two-fold process that must be viewed from the vantage of the group as well as the individual. For the group, socialization is a mechanism through which new members learn the values, norms, knowledge, beliefs, and the interpersonal and other skills that facilitate role performance and further group goals. From the perspective of the individual, socialization is a process of learning to participate in social life. (Mortimer & Simmons, 1978, p. 422)

These authors' definition highlights two different perspectives in the literature on socialization characteristics. In one view, writers have emphasized the organization's goals and processes in molding the newcomer to its definition of what is necessary to do the job and fit into the organization's culture (Baker, 1990; Brim, 1966; Van Maanen & Schein, 1979). These writers describe socialization as ultimately "an influence process leading to organizational control" (Baker, 1990, p. 7). Writers using the other perspective have argued for a more active role for the individual, one in which a person develops an identity that fits with the role and in some cases molds the job (Hall, 1987; G. R. Jones, 1983b; Shackelford, 1992). Although acknowledging that job molding may be limited in its scope, Miller (1988) calls it "a significant process through which work roles are negotiated, involvement is elicited, and the social cohesion necessary for production is maintained" (p. 340). In this book and in the map, we define socialization as a reciprocal process in which both organization and individual are active participants in professional learning.

Content. The content of socialization traditionally includes three processes: (a) developing work skills, (b) adjusting to the work environment, and (c) learning new values (Feldman, 1976). Work socialization is not merely learning the techniques to accomplish the job's tasks. This technical feature of socialization may be the explicit focus, but it is clearly not the only socialization content. For most newcomers, including school administrators, adjusting to the environment is probably the part of the professional journey most fraught with tension and anxiety. This adjustment involves more than getting along with and pleasing a superior; the interaction with faculty and administrative peers may be more important and more burdened with tension.

In addition to learning the tasks and getting along with coworkers and superiors, socialization involves internalizing group values. For organizations to survive and grow, individuals must eventually perform their roles on the basis of an acceptance of norms and values rather than simply compliance with authority (Barnard, 1938). Discovering and internalizing the group's values as well as retaining one's own values are critical parts of socialization.

Writers who use an individual perspective have identified additional socialization content, including personal change in identity, self-image, and motive structure (Fisher, 1986). "To function effectively in a new role, a person must develop a way of viewing himself or herself in that role—a subidentity related to that role" (Hall, 1987, p. 302). The psychosocial function of mentoring focuses on this important socialization content.

Context. A popular newspaper game involves asking readers to locate a larger geographic area by examining a small portion of it. Successful players possess knowledge of local geography—either through visiting the area or studying maps extensively. A stranger to this particular area, however, has difficulty locating the larger context. This game illustrates the difficulty and importance of defining the socialization context. Socialization methods, such as mentoring, occur in a context that may vary in its boundaries. One of the weaknesses of traditional socialization research is the assumption that organizations are bounded, that is, can be clearly defined (Bullis, 1993). Such an assumption risks an overly restricted understanding of socialization.

In the case of principals, we sometimes forget that they are socialized in district, school, work group, and university contexts and therefore mentoring arrangements must acknowledge the learning necessary in these contexts. Since schools are nested in districts and administrators are hired by school boards, principals are socialized to districts as well as schools. As district office agents, principals perform particular administrative tasks. Furthermore, principals must make adjustments in working with superintendents and district office staff and respond to norms and values that are unique to districts, such as experimentation, risk taking, and preferred leadership styles. Finally, principals develop images of themselves in relation to district offices, for example, as agents of the district office, CEOs of the school, or facilitators of faculty (Crow, 1990, 1992).

Equally easy to ignore is the principal's socialization to the subcultures or groups within schools. Until recently, literature on the school administrator's socialization focused exclusively on the profession and ignored the fact that administrators are socialized to an organization, the school (Hart, 1993). We suggest that school administrators are also socialized to and by subcultures within the school, for example, administrator, teacher, parent, and student subcultures.

A mentoring arrangement that, for example, ignores the school's teacher subculture and its influence on an administrative intern not only misses a valuable opportunity for professional learning but risks creating conflicting demands on the intern. Likewise, a mentoring arrangement that ignores the district culture in which a school exists misses the opportunity to help the intern or new administrator develop crucial political skills.

Stages of Socialization

Keeping with our map metaphor, socialization stages are similar to a sequence of map pages outlining a journey. This map arrangement has both advantages and disadvantages. It provides a sequence to the journey, standardizing the routes to take, but it makes the entire journey difficult to view as a whole.

In this section, we discuss the traditional model of socialization stages and briefly identify criticisms of this model. The traditional model includes three stages: anticipatory, encounter, and adjustment. Although the terminology may differ, these three sets of developmental tasks are typically held as the major socialization stages (Hart, 1993).

Anticipatory: Stranger. During the anticipatory stage, the individual is an outsider or stranger in the new profession or organization, for example, as a principal intern. At the point that the individual considers and chooses the job or group, socialization begins. Individuals begin to take on the group's values, which aids their entry into the group and eases adjustment once they are inside (Merton, 1968).

Anticipatory socialization occurs primarily through interaction with individuals acquainted with the role or organization. This interaction becomes more intense as an individual nears "boundary points" (Van Maanen, 1976), gaining the job or entering the organization. The important task at this stage is to develop expectations regarding the job and group.

Encounter: From Stranger to Newcomer. The second stage of the traditional model takes place upon entry into the job and organization. Hughes (1959) referred to the "reality shock" that occurs as one's expectations developed during the anticipatory stage collide with the actual experience in the job. The severity of the shock depends on how inaccurate or unrealistic the expectations are.

Louis (1980a) argued that the surprises, which occur as anticipations and experiences collide, can involve the job, organization, or self. To respond to the surprise, individuals attempt to make sense of new jobs or organizations through their past experiences, personality characteristics, and cultural assumptions and others' information and interpretation. Yet, using someone else's interpretation is problematic, since we filter the information through our past experiences. Similar to interpreting a new map by using traveling experiences in other locales, our past experiences may help us find our way or get us lost. "Until newcomers develop accurate internal maps of the new setting, until they appreciate local meanings, it is important that they have information available for amending internal cognitive maps and for attaching meaning to such surprises as may arise during early job experiences" (Louis, 1980a, p. 244). Mentors and other insiders can be extremely useful in helping the new administrator develop these maps.

Adjustment: From Newcomer to Insider. Adjustment occurs when newcomers become insiders and "are given broad responsibilities and autonomy, entrusted with 'privileged' information" (Louis, 1980a, p.231). The transition to this stage is made apparent through outward signs. "With this transition often comes titles, symbols of status, extra rights or prerogatives, sharing of confidential information or other things which in one way or another indicate that the new member has earned the trust of the organization" (Schein, 1968/1988, p. 58).

The problems of the encounter stage—learning tasks, establishing interpersonal relationships, clarifying roles, and evaluating progress (Feldman, 1976)—are resolved and the individual feels a sense of self-confidence. Feldman found that "many employees reported feeling that until such time as they became friendly and could trust coworkers, they could not find out information that was essential to them to do their jobs well" (p. 442).

Criticisms of Traditional Stage Models. Although some researchers have found evidence of different types of learning occurring during the socialization process (e.g., Feldman, 1976), others have found "no evidence for distinct stages which are the same in terms of order, duration, and content for all jobs or all people" (Fisher, 1986, p. 119; see also Adkins, 1990). Three major criticisms of the traditional model have been identified, which are useful in our development of a socialization map.

First, the traditional stage model tends to ignore individual differences and focus almost exclusively on what the organization does to the individual. This view of socialization ignores the past experience, personality characteristics, and cultural assumptions that the individual brings to the socialization process. New principals, whose experiences as assistant principals consisted solely of student management responsibilities, are likely to see their new roles in very different ways from new principals who had broader assistant principal experiences.

A second criticism is the failure to look for changes in the job itself (Fisher, 1986): "All too often the job is treated as a constant, which remains unchanged as the newcomer tries to learn it and alter him or herself to fit it. . . . Stages of job change, as well as changes of individual adjustment, need to be studied" (p. 120). Administrators who become principals of restructuring schools are likely to encounter jobs that are different from those they have experienced in more traditional schools (Crow & Peterson, 1994).

Third, the traditional stage model overlooks ineffective socialization. The model includes the assumption that when individuals complete the last stage of adjustment role conflicts and dilemmas are resolved. This ignores those individuals who do not resolve these tensions, yet remain with the organization. These marginalized individuals may continue to play significant roles in organizations, which has implications for mentoring (Bullis & Stout, 1996).

Methods of Socialization

When we use a map to take a journey, we usually have more than one way to get where we are going. We choose routes depending on various criteria, for example, time, scenery, road conditions, and intermediate destinations. Similar to maps, socialization methods are numerous and assume different goals (destinations).

"There is seemingly no logical or conclusive end to a list of organizational socialization tactics. The list may well be infinite, for these
are essentially cultural forms that are continually subject to inven-
tion and modification as well as stabilization and continuity" (Van
Maanen & Schein, 1979, p. 232). Socialization methods are not uniform across all organizations or occupations, but are shaped by the
unique organizational culture in which they are used. Thus universities, schools, groups, and districts develop methods over time to
reinforce and perpetuate the behaviors, norms, values, and beliefs
that undergird life and work in the profession and group.

To understand socialization methods, we begin with an identification of the types of methods and then turn to a discussion of how
individuals influence those methods. Our attempt is obviously not
to provide an exhaustive list of socialization strategies but to illustrate the way methods are used to socialize individuals to roles,
groups, organizations, and occupations.

Types of Methods. Socialization methods can be divided into "first
wave" methods, which include the training and education received
by an individual prior to joining an organization, and "second
wave" methods, which are the strategies used by organizations,
groups, and occupations after an individual's entrance to an organization (Inkeles, 1969). In this section, we concentrate on "second
wave" methods, because mentoring occurs primarily after organizational entrance.

Van Maanen and Schein (1979) developed their classic typology
of socialization methods based on the "boundary passages" that individuals make as they move hierarchically (up the organizational
ladder), functionally (to different departments or task areas), or in
terms of inclusionary boundaries (toward or away from central
power relationships). These authors identified six major categories
of socialization tactics, represented as extremes of a continuum: collective versus individual; formal versus informal; sequential versus
random socialization; fixed versus variable; serial versus disjunctive; and investiture versus divestiture.

First distinguished by Becker (1964), collective socialization
methods involve putting newcomers through a common set of experiences, whereas individual socialization isolates the newcomers.
The formal versus informal category was first used by Cogswell

(1968) for the degree to which newcomers are segregated from the work setting for a period of time during their training (Fisher, 1986). Sequential versus random socialization refers to the degree to which "a given sequence of discrete and identifiable steps leading to the target role" are provided (Van Maanen & Schein, 1979, p. 241). Fixed versus variable methods describe the degree to which the steps in the learning process follow a set timetable.

Serial versus disjunctive socialization methods, first identified by Wheeler (1966), refer to whether or not veteran organizational members are available and used to groom newcomers. Mentoring is typically categorized as a kind of serial socialization method because veteran administrators serve as mentors. The actual process of mentoring, however, involves methods from several categories.

Investiture versus divestiture socialization processes, first developed by Schein (1964) in his description of "upending experiences," refer to the ways organizations acknowledge the newcomer's skills and values. For example, mentoring arrangements that celebrate and utilize the newcomer's prior experience illustrate investiture. In contrast, mentoring arrangements designed to strip away characteristics from earlier socialization, as when new principals are expected to break their alliances with teachers, involve divestiture.

More recently, Jones (1986) adapted Van Maanen and Schein's (1979) six categories to develop a new typology (see Hart, 1993, for application of Jones's typology to principal succession). Jones presented three categories of tactics, including context, in which the organization provides information to newcomers; content, which refers to the information given to newcomers; and social or interpersonal aspects of socialization, which includes the interpretations of other organizational members.

Various writers focus on socialization strategies that communicate cultural norms, values, and beliefs. A classic way to distinguish these methods is Van Gennep's (1909/1960) three rites of passage. Rites of separation are the methods used to "detach people, often physically as well as symbolically, from their former roles and move them symbolically into a transitional or 'betwixt-and-between' phase" (Trice, 1993, p. 118). Rites of transition are the methods used "when the past has lost its grip and the future has not yet taken definite shape" (Turner, 1970, p. 354). Rites of incorporation are methods used to signal that the individual is now an insider, as in, for example, giving keys to an intern. Trice (1993) and others focus on the rites, rituals, ceremonies, and stories that are the cultural methods occupations and groups use to influence these passages.

Clearly, the organization or work group intentionally or unintentionally creates and uses socialization methods to accomplish particular types of professional learning for the newcomer. Individuals are not passive in this process, however.

Individual Influences. Four examples of how individuals influence socialization methods are personal characteristics (e.g., gender), previous experience, attitudes (e.g., self-efficacy), and sources of information. Men and women approach the task of identifying and attaching to others in different ways (Hall, 1987). Hall argued that men tend to be socialized through separation and the development of autonomy, whereas women tend to develop their sense of self through relationships, attachments, and caring. Such differences are likely to make the socialization process and the perceptions of socialization methods look very different for men and women. As we discuss in subsequent chapters, these gender differences influence the socialization methods at different career stages.

The influence of the newcomer's previous experience is critical for understanding socialization methods and processes. From the organization's perspective, if the newcomer's previous experience is aligned with the values of the organization, the socialization methods involve reaffirming these values. If the previous experience, however, is not aligned with the organization's values, the methods are more likely to involve a "destructive or unfreezing phase" (Schein, 1968/1988, pp. 54-55). From the individual's perspective, "cultures of orientation" developed in previous roles "help shape their understandings and responses to the task demands and performance requirements made of them in any new setting" (Van Maanen, 1984, p. 217).

Along with personal characteristics and previous experience, individuals' attitudes may affect their perceptions of socialization methods and influence the goals of socialization. Personality factors, such as "desire for control" or "desire for feedback" (Nicholson, 1984), hardiness (Hall, 1987), self-concept, character traits, motivation (Van Maanen, 1976), tolerance for organizational influence (Schein & Ott, 1962), and self-efficacy (Jones, 1986), have been investigated as influences on the socialization process. G. R. Jones (1983b), for example, argued that the strength of self-efficacy expectations is directly related to newcomers' perceptions of their success in dealing with past situations and their anticipated success in the future.

Sources, variety, and availability of information and feedback also influence the socialization process. Rather than sitting idly by waiting to experience the organization's socialization methods, newcomers actively seek information and feedback from a variety of sources, for example, spouses, friends, and coworkers (Akerlund, 1988; Fisher, 1986).

> Socialization is a two way street. On one side, the organization tries to indoctrinate newcomers to its way of thinking and to have newcomers meet its expectations. On the other side, newcomers evaluate the extent to which the organization meets their expectations. To some degree, newcomers and the organization influence each other's expectations. (London, 1985, p. 34)

Goals of Socialization

Returning to our journey metaphor, the primary reason for using a map is to reach a destination. But journeys have other types of goals in addition to reaching a destination. On many journeys the process of traveling rather than the destination is the most memorable part of the trip. One of us took a group of 2- and 3-year-olds on a field trip to see Christmas decorations and visit Santa Claus. When the children returned and were asked by their parents what they saw, the children replied excitedly, "We rode a bus!"

Focus of Goals. When we examine the goals of socialization, what happens to individuals tends to be emphasized. As we will see, the organization and role are also likely to change in the socialization process (Baker, 1990; Geuss, 1993).

Socialization goals can intend changes in the individual's knowledge, behavior, attitudes, beliefs, and personal values related to the organization, the group, the job, and self (Fisher, 1986). The complexity and importance of each of these goals of course differs with the kind of organization, group, and job, as well as the characteristics of the individual. Fisher reminds us that socialization is not simply learning how to perform the techniques of the job.

In addition to individual changes, the actual roles that people perform change. Roles may change in terms of their knowledge base, strategy, and mission (Van Maanen & Schein, 1979). These role features change because of environmental or societal problems; role succession where the individual has a different style than the predecessor; and deliberate attempts, as by universities, to change the profession (Hart, 1993; Schein, 1971b). For example, recent educational reforms describe restructuring environments that require the redefinition of school administration roles (Crow & Peterson, 1994; Odden, 1995).

Organizations also change through the socialization process. Anyone who has survived a hiring process is well aware of how individual characteristics of newcomers can shape various features of the organization. Educational organizations make room for newcomers they value by adding new structures (e.g., courses or course levels), adapting procedures (e.g., giving reduced teaching loads to newcomers), and adjusting reward systems (e.g., giving extra-curricular assignments to adjust the pay of newcomers).

Although organization culture is typically extremely stable, surface and even deep changes can occur, such as when a large number of newcomers with similar values enter the organization at one time. In addition, the effect of individuals with different needs and characteristics over time can affect the organization's tone. School effectiveness research clearly identified the effect that, for example, burned-out teachers can have over time on the school's culture and effectiveness (Teddlie & Stringfield, 1993).

The socialization process not only opens the individual up for change but is a critical point in the organization's life cycle. As schools (and subcultures within them) attempt to "unfreeze" individuals to make them open to the school's norms, values, and beliefs, these organizations place themselves in the vulnerable position of having to examine their own values, norms, and beliefs. For example, the school's (or veteran teacher subculture's) view of innovation and risk taking may change depending on the gifts and talents of the newcomer.

Types of Goals. Merton (1968) identified five types of individual adaptation to socialization to the larger culture: conformity, innovation, ritualism, retreatism, and rebellion. Based on Merton's work, Schein (1968/1988) identified the following types of responses to socialization based on the acceptance or rejection of pivotal, relevant, and peripheral values and norms of the organization or profession. Rebellion involves the rejection of all values and norms, whereas conformity entails the acceptance of all values and norms. Creative individualism necessitates the acceptance only of the pivotal values and norms and the rejection of others. An assistant principal who accepts the need to maintain control but rejects the idea of an authoritarian approach to controlling students illustrates creative individualism.

Schein's (1971b) well-known typology is based on the three features of roles identified earlier: knowledge base, strategy, and mission. He identified three types of role orientation that we can identify as goals of socialization: custodianship, content innovation, and role innovation. Custodianship involves the total acceptance of the knowledge base, strategic practices, and mission as determined by the profession or organization. Content innovation is characterized by the "acceptance of the traditional norms of the profession pertaining to practice, but by a dissatisfaction with the existing levels of knowledge and skill which underlie the profession" (p. 522). Role innovation involves a rejection of the profession's typical practices and a concern with changing the profession's mission.

Literature on these types of socialization goals have raised two major issues: conformity and success of socialization. Organizations tend to be concerned with underconformity, that is, newcomers not acquiring the necessary knowledge, skills, norms, and values to enable them to do the job and commit themselves to the organization. Several researchers (Feldman, 1981; Fisher, 1986; Long, 1988; Schein, 1968/1988), however, voiced concern that overconformity can be dysfunctional to the individual and the organization. Van Maanen and Schein (1979) argued that conformity may be desirable in some organizational settings, for example, for bank tellers, grocery baggers, and members of marching bands. Overconformity may be dysfunctional for schools because they need innovation to adapt to environmental demands.

Successful socialization is usually defined in terms of the individual's proficiency in the skills necessary for a particular stage and whether the individual has completed all socialization stages. If successful socialization is defined only from the school or district perspective as successfully acquiring the knowledge, skills, and norms to do the job, is this functional? Or is it possible for an administrator to be successfully socialized but dysfunctional in terms of helping the school adapt to new demands?

Relationship Between Methods and Goals. As routes are connected to destinations, so methods are related to goals. Van Maanen and Schein (1979) argued, for example, that serial socialization methods—where veterans are used to perpetuate the norms—lead to custodial role orientations. Jones (1986) found a negative relationship between institutionalized methods (i.e., collective, formal, fixed, sequential, serial, and investiture) and innovative role orientations as well as a positive relationship between individualized methods (individual, informal, variable, random, disjunctive, and divestiture) and innovative orientations.

Recent research, however, suggests that the relationship between socialization methods and outcomes is moderated by various types of individual, organizational, and role variables. For example, Baker (1990) found that newcomers with less tolerance for organizational influence are less motivated in institutionalized socialization settings. Baker also argued for organizational size as a moderating variable: "Small organizations which are more likely to offer individualized socialization, can also directly encourage motivation with clear performance demands" (p. 100). Role variables may also moderate the socialization-motivation effect. For example, Baker found, "People in positions of greater responsibility are sometimes more likely to be trained in an individualized manner since responsible positions are often unique and unstandardized" (p. 124).

Criticisms of Socialization Literature

The socialization literature previously discussed serves us well in mapping the administrative journey, but it is not without fault. In this section, we summarize five major criticisms in order to develop a socialization model for understanding the context of mentoring.

First, socialization literature tends to emphasize a passive approach to socialization; that is, the organization socializes the individual. Such a deterministic approach ignores the multiple ways individuals resist organizational efforts to mold them into predetermined roles. Individuals, however, do more than resist; they influence organizational efforts. The literature on "role making" highlights the negotiations that occur between individuals and the groups they enter and belong to.

Second, the literature tends to focus solely on "successful" socialization experiences (Bullis & Stout, 1996). Thus, marginalized individuals who do not fit the organizational mold are overlooked as unimportant. Yet, many of these individuals remain with the organization and have considerable influence on the organization, group, and role. Understanding marginalized and ineffective socialization experiences may give us a clearer picture of what happens in the socialization process (Van Maanen, 1976).

Third, socialization literature largely spotlights the entry level—newcomers without prior work experience. This emphasis has led to a devaluing of the effect of previous experience on socialization processes. The focus on "reality shock" (Hughes, 1959) has ignored the ways individuals use their previous experience to understand and negotiate role knowledge, skills, and values. This emphasis on the entry level has also tended to exclude mid-career socialization experiences from attention (with some notable exceptions; see Hart, 1993; Nicholson, 1984; Nicholson & West, 1989). Such an exclusion ignores the career-long nature of socialization.

Fourth, socialization literature has focused on a stereotypical masculine model of career and socialization. Such a model focuses attention on the competitive, achievement side of processes and outcomes and excludes the relationship-building and caring side that recent research in the feminist tradition presents. As this tradition suggests, such an exclusion not only ignores women's socialization experiences but presents an incomplete picture of men's socialization.

Finally, the socialization literature tends to emphasize uniformity of socialization, which results from an assumption about organizational boundaries. When we define organization narrowly as the school or even the district, we ignore the larger institutional context and the smaller group or subculture contexts that influence socialization processes. Individuals are not only socialized to professions and organizations, they are also socialized to societal expectations and subgroup norms.

A Map for the Journey: A Model of Socialization for Mentoring

The previous literature review and critique mapped the mile markers, directions, terrain, routes, and destinations for the administrative journey. In this section, we use those features to present our map of socialization to help us understand how mentoring arrangements fit in the socialization context.

Mile Markers (Time)

One feature of following a map is figuring out how far we have come and how far we have to go. Mile markers, or milestones, serve that purpose. They permit us to divide the journey up so we have a sense of accomplishment and they also enable us to describe our journey: "For the first 100 miles, we traveled through desert; then we passed through 250 miles of mountain ranges."

Socialization occurs over and over throughout our work lives as we take on new positions, new tasks, and new orientations to our work and enter new organizations. School administration is clearly not the occupation it was 20 or even 10 years ago (Beck & Murphy, 1993). Although we may talk about Ms. Jones being a principal for the last 25 years, her practice as a principal has undoubtedly changed during that period.

Mile markers also describe where we have been. The ongoing nature of socialization involves the recognition that prior socialization affects future socialization. The fact that all principals have been teachers or school counselors should not be ignored. The socialization that occurred in learning to teach and the unique teacher orientations that developed are bound to affect the administrative orientations that assistant principals and principals develop.

Time is a critical feature of socialization and therefore of mentoring. The sequence or lack of sequence of learning that occurs is pivotal to reaching the goals of mentoring. The prior experiences of interns, assistant principals, new principals, and veteran principals influence their interpretations of and their responses to mentoring arrangements. Thus, a major feature of our map or model of socialization includes time—as an organizer of mentoring experiences and as an influence on mentoring content, methods, and goals.

Directions (Sources)

For maps to be understood and interpreted, there must be directions. Some code or legend must point to north, south, east, and west. These legends orient us and thereby direct us from where we are to where we want to go.

Socialization is initiated and directed by both the individual and socializing agents. Individuals do not passively wait to be instructed on how to learn their new roles or tasks or how to get to know their coworkers. Clearly, organizations, work groups, occupations, and communities have a stake in initiating and directing the socialization process. Individuals also have an interest in this process. The uncertainty and anxiety (Backer, 1990; Hughes, 1959; Stonehocker, 1992; Wilson, 1986) inherent in beginning a new role and entering a new organization provide enough incentive for newcomers to take an active part in directing their socialization. Not only do individuals direct their socialization by virtue of their motivation, but various characteristics of the individual influence the process. For example, gender, age, experience, and personality variables (e.g., self-efficacy) help to shape and direct socialization.

We are not suggesting that individuals have total control of the socialization process. Clearly, universities, schools, occupational communities (Van Maanen & Barley, 1984), and political communities are powerful socializing agents. They have a stake in making sure that administrative newcomers develop the knowledge, skills, behaviors, and values to do the job, adjust to the work environment, and commit themselves over the long haul.

Sources are critical features of the socialization process who influence the content, methods, and goals of mentoring. Throughout this book we identify the ways individuals and other socializing agents interact in the mentoring process.

Terrain (Content)

Maps that include only roads are slightly more useful than maps that include only country or state boundaries. Maps that tell us what type of terrain, including topology, towns, and landmarks, are extremely useful for making sure we are on the right road and for making the journey considerably more pleasant.

The terrain of socialization includes the two major types of content that professional learning involves: technical and cultural. Newcomers must learn the knowledge and skills necessary to do the job tasks, and they must learn the behaviors and values necessary for adjusting to the work environment and committing themselves to the work and organization. Socialization practices, including those for preparing school administrators, are notorious for emphasizing the technical and ignoring the cultural. Cultural learning for newcomers is as necessary to the successful performance of the job as possessing the knowledge and skills. Throughout this book, we identify the technical and cultural content that aspiring, new, and mid-career administrators must possess to do their jobs in a dynamic leadership orientation and how mentoring can facilitate learning this content.

Routes (Methods)

Useful maps have routes to direct our journey. The routes may be clearly delineated highways with information regarding distances, type of highway, road conditions, and interchanges. Routes may also be less delineated with terrain markers that permit us only to know, for example, mountain passes or water sources. Both types of maps provide routes to destinations but with more or less detail.

Socialization methods, likewise, are more or less delineated in terms of getting us to our destination and helping us along the administrative journey. Mentoring is clearly a serial socialization method (Van Maanen & Schein, 1979), using veterans to pass on knowledge and skills to newcomers. Mentoring is likely to include a cluster of methods that may reinforce or contradict each other. Mentoring does not occur in a vacuum but interacts with other socialization methods at various career stages.

Destinations (Goals)

If a map does not include destinations, we have trouble getting where we want to go or knowing when we get there. Socialization has destinations, or goals. Much of the attention in the literature has been on the process of socialization. But as Van Maanen and Schein (1979) argued, there is a relationship between how we get somewhere and where we end up. If our goal—as individuals or organizations—is to develop administrators who perpetuate the status quo, we must discover those methods most likely to accomplish this. If, on the other hand, we wish to be innovative, our methods will differ.

Throughout the book, we examine socialization and mentoring at various career stages in terms of goals, in particular, developing dynamic leaders for learning communities. As we propose how to implement mentoring, our discussion will connect content, methods, and goals.

A Look Back and a Look Ahead

The socialization features discussed in this chapter create a map that can be used to understand how mentoring for school administrators fits into the larger socialization context. We do not suggest that this is an all-encompassing model. Nor is it a causal model. We believe that the model, like a map, can guide our reflection, practice, and research on mentoring. This map can also help us in developing mentoring arrangements that enhance the socialization of dynamic school leaders.

In the next chapter, we apply this map to the first administrative career stage: principal interns. We use the map to gain an understanding of the socialization process of interns so that we can develop mentoring arrangements for this stage of the administrative journey. We focus our discussion of interns' socialization by introducing Margaret Chatham and her two mentors.

3

Getting Out of the Driveway

First Miles for Administrative Interns

Margaret: Traveler in a Strange Land?

As Margaret Chatham backed out of her driveway and drove to school on the last day of her internship, memories flooded her mind. On the whole, her yearlong internship had been a good experience, at times even enjoyable. She was glad she had decided to take the full-time internship option. Doing so had allowed her to get more experience and be more visible to district administrators. She hoped that would help her career advancement.

Her internship, however, had included some difficult, even embarrassing situations. For example, Ms. Shuker, her first mentor—Margaret never did dare use her first name—introduced her to the faculty by saying, "This is Ms. Chatham, she's a new intern. I hope she lasts longer than the last one." In spite of the introduction, Ms. Shuker had turned out to be nice enough, but Margaret found it difficult to understand Ms. Shuker's expectations and Ms. Shuker was initially reluctant to let Margaret shadow her. Fortunately, Margaret had

Sarah Brown as her second mentor-principal. Sarah was everything Ms. Shuker was not—helpful, engaging, supportive, and willing to share responsibility. When Margaret had a particularly uncomfortable run-in with a parent, Sarah was supportive but allowed Margaret to handle it. Wow, what a learning experience that had been!

Margaret's internship had been the final requirement for her master's degree in educational administration at Midwest State University. Margaret had taught fifth grade for 10 years when her principal approached her about applying for a special administrative preparation program sponsored jointly by the university and the Hanover School District. Margaret decided this was the best time in terms of her professional and personal obligations.

The clinical internship was designed to provide a variety of perspectives and emphasized reflective practice. The major features of the internship included working with two mentors, one in the fall and one in the spring. On Wednesday evenings, interns met as a group along with a university faculty member and a retired principal to discuss their progress, problems, and successes. Ongoing feedback sessions with the mentors were also supposed to occur, although, as Margaret remembered, this only happened with her second mentor.

The fall portion of Margaret's internship took place at King Elementary School, an inner-city school with Ms. Shuker as principal and no assistant principal. The spring portion took place at Tyler Junior High School, a suburban school with Ms. Brown as principal and Mr. Shotts as assistant principal. As Margaret recalled the highlights of these two experiences, she realized what a picture of contrasts these experiences presented.

The experience with Ms. Shuker at King Elementary had been difficult, and at times Margaret felt she did not belong there. In addition to being introduced to the faculty in such a derogatory way, Margaret was given no space of her own. The librarian, whom Margaret had known earlier, took pity and provided a corner table in the library workroom. Margaret's first meeting with Ms. Shuker was cordial enough but also very businesslike. It was obvious that Ms. Shuker was reluctant to give Margaret any significant projects or responsibilities. She had initially agreed to take an intern in order to have additional clerical help in the office. When the university field

director explained the need for regular feedback conferences and opportunities to perform administrative functions, she reluctantly
agreed. When Margaret first met with her, Ms. Shuker said, "I hope
I don't have to lead you around by the nose all the time. I don't have
time to do that."

It was clear to Margaret that she would have to create her own
learning experiences. So she began by contacting a new teacher to
ask if she could practice some supervisory techniques she had
learned in a university class. The teacher she chose was at first reluctant, but when Margaret assured her the supervision would have no
effect on her evaluation review, the teacher agreed. Margaret felt the
experience working with this teacher had been useful to both of
them, but sometimes in a negative way. Very early in the semester,
Ms. Shuker rejected the possibility of any out-of-class time for
Margaret and the teacher to meet. So they had lunch together to discuss Margaret's observations. She also learned from the new teacher
that other teachers were surprised that Margaret included the new
teacher's assessment in their conference. The new teacher said that
apparently Ms. Shuker always conducted teacher conferences as formal, one-way conversations in which she told the teachers what they
were doing right and wrong.

After the third week, Ms. Shuker allowed Margaret to shadow
her for a couple of days. This gave Margaret a sense of the pace of
Ms. Shuker's day. She was amazed at how much time Ms. Shuker
spent in the classrooms, on the playground, in the halls, and in the
cafeteria. Her university classes had emphasized the importance of
an instructional leadership role for the principal, and Margaret was
excited to see this in action. She wished, however, that Ms. Shuker
would permit her to do more than shadow and perform clerical
tasks. She wanted to sit with Ms. Shuker and reflect on what she saw.

As the semester progressed, Margaret was able to interact with
more teachers and staff members. As staff felt more comfortable with
her, they invited her to their classrooms and even sought out her
advice, especially in science education, her area of expertise.

Toward the end of the semester, Ms. Shuker seemed to feel more
comfortable assigning Margaret responsibility. She asked her to handle particular student discipline problems, to which Margaret felt
that she responded well. When Margaret met with her university
advisers and the other interns, she expressed her frustration at being
denied the opportunity to work more with parents and teachers.

With both relief and anxiety, Margaret began the second semester with Sarah Brown at Tyler Junior High School. Although she was glad to have a new mentor and hoped that this would be a better experience, she was anxious because she had never before worked in a junior high setting.

In their first meeting, Sarah made Margaret feel welcome and invited her to join in student, faculty, and parent conferences whenever their schedules permitted. On the first day of the new semester, Sarah called a short early morning faculty meeting at which she introduced Margaret. Margaret still remembered that introduction. "I am very pleased to introduce Ms. Margaret Chatham. She is completing her administrative certification requirements and will be working with us this semester. Ms. Chatham is a longtime teacher in our district, bringing a lot of great science education experience. She will be serving as my assistant and her decisions should be considered comparable to mine. Her office will be in the room next to mine. This week's 'Faculty Notes' includes Margaret's E-mail address and phone extension. I'm sure you'll want to get to know Margaret and take advantage of her expertise." Margaret was both impressed and frightened. What a lot to live up to!

Barely had the faculty meeting ended, when one of the seventh-grade teachers approached Margaret to ask about appropriate dress for the half-day teacher workday on Friday. She asked if it was all right for teachers to wear jeans during the morning when students would be present and told Margaret that they had been allowed to do this in the past. Margaret was caught off guard but tried to "act her part." She told the teacher that she thought this would be fine (based on the teacher's comments and Margaret's home principal's decision regarding workday dress). Margaret said she wanted to check with Ms. Brown first, however. Before she had a chance to do that, the teacher told the principal that Margaret had given them permission to wear jeans on Friday all day. Sarah's response demonstrated that her introductory remarks were more than mere words. She told the teacher, "If that's what Ms. Chatham said, that's my decision as well."

Margaret remembered that this was not the last time the teachers tested her, but she always felt Sarah's support. It was not long before she felt the acceptance of most faculty members. As they got to know her and find out that her science education expertise was useful even in a junior high setting, they frequently invited her to their classrooms and asked for her suggestions on various science projects. Margaret also arranged a field trip to a university genetics laboratory for the eighth-grade science students and teachers.

In contrast to her earlier mentoring experience, Margaret's relationship with Sarah Brown was both broadening and in-depth. Margaret was welcomed in any conference with Sarah. She accompanied Sarah on teacher observations and was involved in difficult student disciplinary conferences, messy teacher conferences, and meetings with irate parents. After phone calls, Sarah would reflect with Margaret on what had happened in the conversation. As the semester progressed, Sarah gave Margaret more responsibility for teacher observation and conferencing. Margaret was surprised to find that teachers at Tyler expected to have a voice in their conferences—quite a different approach from what she had experienced at King.

Margaret also remembered her travels with Sarah to district administrators' meetings. Frequently, they stopped for coffee after the meetings to discuss district politics. Sarah was always open and responsive to Margaret's questions about the "inside scoop" about administrative appointments. Sarah also asked Margaret how her husband and daughters were responding to Margaret's heavier workload.

Sarah allowed Margaret to "solo" on some parent conferences. The one Margaret most remembered was with a parent who was irate at having his son removed from the school soccer team because his grades had fallen below C. The parent threatened to file a grievance with the district office and emphasized his political clout with the superintendent. Margaret calmly stated that this was a district policy but that he certainly could file a grievance. The parent became more irate and finally stated that he wanted to talk with someone who had "real authority." When Margaret and Sarah met with the parent, Sarah stated that Margaret had her full support and was appropriately enforcing district policies. The parent left the meeting upset and went immediately to the superintendent. When the superintendent called to find out details, Sarah described to him how well Margaret had handled the situation.

As she drove to her last day at Tyler Junior High School, these contrasts between her two internships and mentors seemed so dramatic. She had said to some of the other interns that she probably would not know how great a mentor Sarah was if she had not experienced Ms. Shuker and she certainly knew which style she preferred.

Socialization of Administrative Interns

Margaret's administrative journey as an intern illustrates some of the features of socialization at this beginning stage. Although intern socialization experiences have certain features in common with those at other career stages or "boundary crossings," intern experiences are unique in other respects. Mentoring administrative interns is therefore both similar and unique to mentoring at other stages. In this chapter, we identify the socialization features of administrative interns following the map developed in Chapter 2.

Mile Markers

In some respects, Margaret's administrative journey has just begun. She has received the training and now the clinical experiences to enable her to perform administrative tasks. Learning to cope with the work environment and developing the organizational values and beliefs in her first administrative appointment are still to come. Yet, in other respects, Margaret has been anticipating this journey for years. Anticipatory socialization provides critical mile markers for interns' socialization. Professional and organizational socialization provide important mile markers as well at this stage.

Anticipatory Socialization. The first socialization stage involves "the acquisition of values and orientations found in statuses and groups in which one is not yet engaged but which one is likely to enter" (Merton, 1968, p. 438). Administrative interns have been undergoing a serial socialization process before they became interns. Lortie (1975) estimated that before individuals become teachers they have observed other teachers approximately 13,000 hours. Administrators teach on the average 10 years before entering administration (*Schools and Staffing Survey—1993-1994*, 1993). Assuming this amount of teaching experience, the intern would have experienced hundreds of hours of observing administrators. Although much of this observation does not permit views "behind the scenes," this is a significant amount of time to develop role expectations.

These expectations include a variety of role features, such as the freedom, responsibility, and autonomy available in the role; career advancement potential; the chance to make a significant contribution;

and the characteristics of coworkers and the work atmosphere (Louis, 1978). These expectations form the basis for the degree of "surprise" (Louis, 1980a) that interns experience once they obtain administrative positions.

Three mile markers that occur during the anticipatory socialization period influence the "perspective" (Becker, Geer, Hughes, & Strauss, 1961; Greenfield, 1977a, 1977b) that interns develop before they become administrators. First, previous teaching experience affects the expectations, perspectives, and relationships of principal interns. The transition from teaching to administration is characterized by both direct investiture and indirect divestiture (Greenfield, 1985a). Investiture celebrates the value of skills developed in earlier teaching experience, such as Margaret's science education background, which helped her relate to the teachers.

Divestiture also occurs as particular perspectives on the teacher's role are stripped away, for example, orientation to the classroom. "As the candidate begins to do some of the scut-work (that which many teachers refuse to do or which they dislike doing—monitoring, helping out in the evenings, being a 'go-for' or assisting administrators with many major and minor projects), the teacher 'self' is gradually shed and the administrator 'self' evolves" (Greenfield, 1985a, p. 14).

Second, in addition to previous teaching experience, another mile marker occurs when interns actively participate in their own anticipatory socialization. Long (1988) labeled the activity "positioning and learning" when teachers pursue administration and begin activities to gain visibility and exposure, which results in leaving the teacher group and aligning with the administrative group. "GASing," or "getting the attention of superiors," is a process whereby the teacher or intern seeks to gain visibility and thereby sponsorship into administrative positions (Greenfield, 1977a, 1977b). We discuss the specific ways interns use this activity in the section on methods.

A third mile marker occurs for some interns when they are "tapped" or sponsored. At this point, an administrator encourages them to obtain course work necessary for administrative certification. Traditionally, this has occurred for men more often than for women (Ortiz, 1982; Shakeshaft, 1987). This tapping event makes the individual sensitive to anticipatory socialization cues about what administrators do and value.

Professional Socialization. A second group of mile markers for administrative interns involves the socialization to the occupation that occurs primarily through university training. Professional socialization includes courses and field-based experiences designed to help interns develop an administrative perspective. Recent attempts to reform the educational administration occupation have focused on the importance of clinical field experiences and the need to revitalize these experiences (Griffiths, Stout, & Forsyth, 1988).

An internship experience, at its best, provides opportunities for the intern to obtain a sense of role tasks and values. Developing a sense of the tasks involves not only finding out what the responsibilities are, but gaining a feel for the pace and rhythm of the administrator's day—the brevity, variety, and fragmentation (Peterson, 1977-1978). Although interns have observed administrators for many hours, much of this time has consisted of "on-stage," public appearances by administrators rather than their "behind the scenes" activity. In effective clinical experiences, interns have the opportunity to "shadow" administrators, thereby obtaining a more in-depth understanding of the tasks.

Internships also provide the opportunity to develop a sense of the occupational culture. What kinds of things are important to administrators? What are the values, beliefs, and assumptions of the role? These questions refer to the occupational perspective, "the patterns of thought and action which have grown up in response to a specific set of institutional pressures" (Becker et al., 1961, p. 36).

Organizational Socialization. A third group of mile markers occurs when the principal intern sets foot inside a school as part of the clinical experience. Interns are socialized not only by university faculty and assigned mentors but by other administrators, teachers, students, and parents in the internship school. As Margaret discovered in her second internship, teachers and parents play a major part in socializing a newcomer, even one who will probably leave the school.

Cordeiro and Smith-Sloan (1995) identified five stages in an internship transition model. These take place inside the internship school and highlight the organizational socialization mile markers during this period. At the "initial contact stage," interns are still functioning from the perspective of their old roles and view the internship school from the viewpoint of their home school environment. They are curious and excited but relate to the mentor on a formal basis. During the "liminal stage," interns feel uncomfortable and apprehensive about their ability to perform certain functions and grieve over leaving their previous school. The relationship between the mentor and intern is cautious. During the "settling-in stage," the intern feels more control over time, feels more accepted by the adults in the new school, and relates more openly with the mentor. The "efficacy stage" involves greater feelings of confidence and autonomy and increased creativity and competence in assigned projects. The relationship with the mentor is characterized by sharing and mutual respect. During the final, "independence stage," interns realize there is little more to learn in this context but thoughts of leaving cause a sense of loss. Mentors and interns relate as colearners.These stages suggest that the internship period is one in which features of the new school environment are potent forces for socializing the intern.

Directions

At this stage of Margaret's administrative journey, several organizations and people provided direction. University professors, university student peers, school and district administrators, teachers, students, and parents all potentially influenced the administrative perspective Margaret was developing. Margaret also influenced the direction of her administrative journey.

University Socialization Agents. University preparation in most states consists of courses and clinical field experiences. Courses present theory and research related to broad areas of administration and leadership. Internships permit opportunities on school sites to perform administrative tasks. These two features of university preparation present a major and potentially conflicting socialization source for interns.

Conflict can occur if university socialization agents are inconsistent in their directions to interns. University faculty tend to concentrate on the future role more so than the reality of the current role as it is practiced (Mortimer & Simmons, 1978). Mentors—as practitioners—tend to focus on the role as it currently exists (Schein, 1968/1988). Consistency between university faculty and mentors is important for reinforcing the values, norms, and beliefs that interns develop (Ondrack, 1975).

The role of peers in university training received some early attention, but little contemporary research on this source has occurred. "Peers often form a cohesive group that inculcates norms in direct opposition to the goals of the authorities" (Mortimer & Simmons, 1978, p. 437). Although faculty focus on the formal aspects of the role, peers communicate the informal aspects. Increasingly, administrator preparation programs use cohort arrangements in which students enter and proceed through the program in groups. Although cohorts may reinforce the norms being introduced to prospective administrators, some research suggests that they may also conflict with these norms (Becker et al., 1961; Crow & Glascock, 1995).

Other Socialization Agents. In addition to university faculty, mentors, and peers, interns receive direction and influence from other agents, especially when they enter their internship schools. We focus on three sources of socialization for interns: administrators, teachers, and individuals outside the school.

Obviously, district and school administrators provide major direction for the intern. They constitute the administrative reference group and thus have significant power in the socialization process. Interns at this stage turn to members of the administrative group for knowledge and advice not only about the role tasks but about the nature of candidacy and mobility (Greenfield, 1977a, 1977b). In most internship programs, the intern is in closest proximity to school administrators. These administrators are in the best position to help reduce the uncertainty that new recruits experience by clarifying concerns, answering questions, checking perceptions, and acquainting interns with school culture (Falcione & Wilson, 1988).

District administrators also serve as agents of socialization. Since they usually make the final decision to hire administrators, they have a stake in grooming interns to fit the administrative perspective regarded as appropriate in the district (Baltzell & Dentler, 1983).

In addition to administrators, teachers serve as socializing agents for interns. The direction provided by teachers for administrative socialization has been largely ignored in the literature, partly because the typical view is that interns begin to separate from the teacher culture (Ortiz & Marshall, 1988). As interns do the "dirty work" that teachers do not want to do, they begin to identify less with teachers and more with administrators (Greenfield, 1977a, 1977b). Administrative socialization involves passing muster with two new cultures: the new school setting and the world of administrative peers and superiors (Ortiz & Marshall, 1988). This process begins during the internship as teachers test the intern's competency, instructional orientation, and alliances (as in Margaret's early experience with the teacher who asked about appropriate dress) (Crow & Pounders, 1996). Teachers' importance as a socialization source is also apparent in the fact that interns spend time, especially early in their internships, doing things for teachers to develop good working relationships (Cordeiro & Smith-Sloan, 1995; Crow & Pounders, 1996).

Family and friends also influence the socialization process by their images of the role and by their demands on the intern's time during the internship. Cordeiro and Smith-Sloan (1995) identified the "grieving" process that many interns described in feeling that they were cheating their families due to time demands. This process may affect later perspectives about how to balance work and family roles.

Although all these socialization agents can be potentially important sources of intern socialization, they no doubt vary in their importance and in the nature of their influence. Two aspects of the intern/socialization agent relationship affect the importance of these sources: power and affectivity (Brim, 1966). Power involves the degree to which the agent exerts dominance or authority in the relationship. Obviously, administrators have formal authority over the intern, but teachers and outsiders can exert dominance depending on the socialization issue. Affectivity involves the feelings between the socialization agent and the intern and is the most important aspect of the relationship in developing the values, norms, and beliefs of the role (Greenfield, 1985c). It is clear that although the power of Margaret's two mentors may have been similar, the affectivity was not.

Conflict Between Professional and Organizational Socialization. A potential conflict exists between professional socialization and organizational socialization as interns enter their internship schools. "Schools [graduate schools] socialize their students toward a concept of a profession, organizations socialize their new members to be effective members" (Schein, 1968/1988, p. 54). Professional socialization may effectively socialize the newcomer to job-related skills and knowledge but may inhibit developing insider beliefs about the job (Adkins, 1990).

Interns are simultaneously being socialized in professional and organizational contexts. Both contexts have values, norms, and beliefs about school administration and both attempt to socialize interns to their particular values. We suggest that the response to such conflict is not to make the norms and values identical between the two contexts but to acknowledge the importance of both. Interns need to know both what the future role of the administrator can be and what current reality is. Mentoring can help bridge this gulf.

Individual Influence. Our previous discussion may suggest that university, district, and school personnel are the only socialization sources and that interns are relatively passive. Interns provide direction, however, for their own socialization.

Several characteristics of individuals influence socialization, including previous experience, personality characteristics, and gender differences. Earlier in this chapter, we discussed how previous experience, especially in teaching, can influence the socialization of new interns. The long serial socialization process that interns experience affects the role perspectives they develop. Personality characteristics, such as toleration for organizational influence (Schein & Ott, 1962), are also likely to affect the intern's socialization experience in terms of openness to various professional and organizational influences.

Gender differences are receiving more attention. Although the length of teaching experiences among men and women is more similar than in the past, women tend to teach longer than men (12.6 years for women and 9.3 years for men; *Schools and Staffing Survey—1993-1994,* 1993). Such variation may create differences in the norms and values toward instruction that have been formed over long versus short tenures as teachers.

Invitation to apply for administrative positions also influences the socialization process differently for women versus men. Nelson (1986) found that men received specific communications telling them they would be "perfect" for the position. Although women received encouragement from men to apply, it was subtle in nature. Generally, women had to find their own opportunities and be discreet in seeking opportunities. Ortiz (1982) found that female teachers were cautious about showing their ability and learned not to show any administrative aspiration before tenure. These features reduce women's GASing (getting the attention of superiors) behavior, making them less visible and open to administrative perspectives and sponsorship. Turoczy (1996) found that women were less likely than men to be sponsored for administrative positions.

The graduate school experience may be different for women and men. Shakeshaft and Hanson (1986) point to the male bias in educational administration literature, which stresses male perspectives and affects preparation program curricula.

Terrain

The terrain of Margaret's administrative journey during the internship period blended professional and organizational socialization. She had to learn not only to identify with an occupation but to live—albeit temporarily—in an organization. The knowledge, skills, behaviors, and values she learned in her university training were tested, refined, adjusted, and perhaps abandoned when she worked in the two internship schools.

Two types of learning are required in the intern's identification with the occupation: technical and cultural (Greenfield, 1985c). Technical learning is focused on the instrumental side of the role: acquiring and appropriately using the knowledge and skills required to perform role tasks. Cordeiro and Smith-Sloan (1995) found that interns in their study reported four major areas of learning: basic knowledge about day-to-day building operations, strategies for information collection and problem solving, effective ways to work with a variety of adults, and ways to manage their time given multiple tasks. One of the tasks for interns and their mentors is to distinguish the generic from the specific, that is, what knowledge and skills are necessary to perform the administrative role regardless of setting and what knowledge and skills are context specific.

The second type of content learned in the internship is cultural (or moral) learning, which includes sentiments, beliefs, standards of practice, and value orientations. This type of learning is unfortunately rarely discussed in university training programs (Greenfield, 1985c). Yet, understanding the values, norms, beliefs, and assumptions that undergird the occupation and the organization are critical to "living" this work.

Margaret's experience in the case study confirms the importance of cultural learning. Her experiences with not only mentors but teachers and parents suggest that these norms and values may vary with the particular school subcultures. For example, teachers' norms of equity and fairness are critical for the intern to learn. Interns apparently understand the importance of these cultural learnings, as they intently and energetically attempt to form relationships with teachers and students (Crow & Pounders, 1996).

An important part of the socialization content of the internship is developing an administrative perspective. Greenfield (1985a) identified four dimensions of work context that are critical features of an administrative perspective: relations with teachers, relations with community, relations with peers and superiors, and the necessity to establish or develop routines associated with organizational stability and the maintenance of smooth daily operations.

Routes

Margaret's administrative journey during this internship stage consisted of a variety of routes for acquiring the knowledge, skills, behaviors, and values necessary for identifying with administration. Some of the routes were clearly marked and obvious in their purpose, for example, shadowing the mentor; others were more subtle, such as testing by the teacher regarding appropriate clothing. In this section, we begin with a general description of the socialization methods used by the occupation, organization, and individual during the internship stage. We then describe some specific methods used to teach technical and cultural learning.

General Methods of the Internship. The transition from teaching to administration is individual, informal, random, variable, and serial and involves both investiture and divestiture (Greenfield, 1985a). Greenfield argued that in most cases prospective administrators design their own candidacy strategy rather than follow a collective approach. In those cohort programs currently being used in innovative preparation programs, individual strategies are still in place. The transition from teaching to administration is also informal; that is, no formal designation of candidate is given. Furthermore, the transition is random, with few clear steps regarding the process and progress toward reaching administrative appointment, and variable, in that candidates usually are hard pressed to know where they stand. The transition involves the importance of role incumbents passing on the learning (serial). Finally, the process is typically characterized as involving both divestiture—efforts to strip away the teacher perspective—and investiture—confirming the worth and appropriateness of certain value orientations, skills, and attitudes.

The intern, however, does not passively wait to be molded by the organization, but may use a very active process. GASing involves methods that interns use to promote their candidacy and learn the administrative perspective.

Greenfield (1977a, 1977b) distinguished interns on the basis of their GASing behavior that influenced the breadth of their administrative perspective. He found that some interns were assertive in their GASing behavior, testing limits, exploiting resources, and controlling structure. Others were more complacent in their GASing behavior, assuming limits, using an affective orientation (rather than an instrumental orientation) toward others, and accepting structure. The assertive interns were also more likely to interact with administrators and to "show off" their skills and knowledge, whereas complacent interns were reluctant to do so and saw such behavior as "brownnosing." As a result, the assertive interns developed a fuller administrative perspective, defined as one oriented toward the entire school rather than an individual classroom. These methods involve the active participation of the individual intern in the socialization process by allowing the intern to control the kind and amount of learning that occurs.

Specific Methods for Technical Learning. University preparation is designed to teach some technical skills necessary for performing the administrative role. Courses in budgeting, supervision, law, and staff development teach skills necessary for the role. The internship also teaches these skills through the clinical experience in a school and with a mentor. Cordeiro and Smith-Sloan (1995) found that the typical pattern for internship learning involved scaffolding: observe, talk through, reflect, and do. In this process, mentors acted as guides. These researchers also found that mentors were more directive in the early stages of the internship, "staggering" or "chunking" activities and paperwork (p.18).

Specific Methods for Cultural Learning. Whereas university training primarily involves technical learning, preparation programs are beginning to recognize that courses designed to help interns analyze organizations, reflect on their leadership, and understand organizational politics aid in cultural as well as technical learning. These courses, especially when taught with simulations such as case studies, provide the intern with understanding of and sensitivity to the values and norms of the occupation and organization.

At the clinical internship level, cultural learning is a major priority. Two conditions have been associated with administrators' moral (cultural) socialization (Greenfield, 1985c). First, the role orientation of the immediate supervisor is a major method for inculcating these norms and values. Observing and interacting with a mentor or other administrator in terms of what is acceptable, what is important and what may be ignored, what requires attention and what does not, what is viewed as problematic and what is not, and what action alternatives are and are not acceptable (Greenfield, 1985c, p. 104) socializes the intern to occupational and organizational values. The second condition associated with moral socialization includes the dominant work activities associated with learning and performing the administrative role. Stability is viewed as a major priority among most administrators (Greenfield, 1985c). Activities that promote the maintenance of smooth daily operations are deemed critical and emphasize administrative perspectives that include this stability.

Other socialization methods used to teach cultural learning also exist. Crow and Pounders (1996) identified several methods used to help interns "learn the ropes" of an occupational culture. These included major cultural forms: artifacts (keys to building, office space), rituals (early bombardment of responsibility and shadowing), rites (selection process and testing by faculty), and ceremonies (introduction to the faculty). Clearly, these had both manifest and latent levels of learning. They taught clearly overt technical requirements for the job, and, just as important, they taught at the latent level the underlying assumptions and beliefs that undergird the administrator's role.

Destinations

The administrative journey that Margaret began with her experiences with two mentors will continue with various goals. Some of those goals are immediately apparent, for example, her increased pragmatism in regard to the tasks and effects of the role. Others are goals that will not be seen until she enters her first administrative appointment. In this section, we identify two types of goals of principal

intern socialization: those associated with their professional socialization and those of a more general nature.

Goals of Professional Socialization. The professional socialization of
interns has been primarily viewed as a transition from idealism to a
pragmatic orientation (Becker et al., 1961; O'Brien, 1988; Ondrack,
1975). The idealism that caused individuals to prepare for school administration is tempered during the internship with the *variety, brevity,* and *fragmentation* of the role and by a beginning realization of the
limits of the administrator's effects. This pragmatic orientation begins to refine expectations in order to lessen the "surprise" (Louis,
1980a) of initial entry.

Within this more pragmatic orientation lies the possibility for
more subtle goals. Schein (1971b) identified two types of professional schools (universities), custodial and innovative, that inculcate
different norms and expectations regarding the role. The norms
learned in an innovative graduate program can be either enhanced
or undone by the organizational socialization that occurs early in the
career. Socialization outcomes in an innovative university setting
can be undone if processes during the internship and early career are
not acknowledged and the personnel in universities, districts, and
schools do not work together.

Other Types of Socialization Goals. In Chapter 2, we distinguished
three socialization goals based on the work of Merton (1968) and
Schein (1968/1988): conformity, rebellion, and creative individualism. All three of these goals are possible in intern socialization.

Conformity is probably the most likely to occur given the typical
methods of socializing interns (Greenfield, 1985a). In addition, one
of the major aspects of the work context that is critical to an administrative perspective is the maintenance of stability and smooth daily
operations (Greenfield, 1977a, 1977b). Although stability may be especially important in schools that have undergone radical change in
the community, stability as a long-term and singular purpose is dysfunctional for schools that must respond to a changing environment.

Rebellion is probably the least likely goal of intern socialization.
By the time an individual reaches the intern stage, a significant
amount of self- and organizational selection, sponsorship, and filter-
ing have occurred (Greenfield, 1977a, 1977b; Ortiz, 1982). The possibility of rebellion against preparation program values still exists.

Crow and Glascock (1995), in a study of an internship program designed to prepare more democratic leaders, found evidence of rebellion. When interns were interviewed at the end of the program, they expressed aspirations for "taking charge," that is, molding schools to fit their ideas of what is needed by disadvantaged urban youngsters. Their views were clearly in opposition to the espoused purposes of the preparation program. What partially explained the researchers' finding is the passionate commitment to the betterment of urban youngsters that these interns brought with them from extensive urban teaching experience. Their previous experience, as well as their cohort and internship experience, led to a view opposed by program planners.

A third type of goal, creative individualism, is based on the acceptance of pivotal values of the organization or occupation but the rejection of peripheral ones. Such a goal may occur if interns have socialization experiences, such as mentorships, that emphasize consistent pivotal goals, such as working toward the creation of a community of learners, and the opportunity to see those goals enacted in multiple ways. Having more than one mentor may encourage diversity of perspectives that would engender creative individualism among interns.

Before leaving the discussion of socialization goals at this internship stage of the administrative journey, it is important to acknowledge the existence of ineffective socialization at this stage (Bullis & Stout, 1996; Van Maanen, 1976). Clearly interns can have weak university courses and weak internship programs. If Margaret's entire internship experience had been with Ms. Shuker, who was unwilling or unable to delegate responsibility to Margaret, the outcome would clearly be less effective than it probably was with both mentors involved.

Crow and Pounders (1996) found that all interns did not experience the same rites, rituals, and ceremonies. Some were introduced to the faculty in derogatory ways that deemphasized their authority and lowered expectations. Some were not given roles to play or delegated responsibility. These interns clearly indicated that they felt unprepared for the administrative role—they felt marginalized and isolated. Many of these will never become administrators because of the lack of sponsorship. Others will obtain appointments through some other means but continue to be marginalized in the administrative group.

A Look Back and a Look Ahead

We have set the context for the first part of the administrative journey using the map developed in Chapter 2. The socialization of interns creates the context in which the mentoring of interns exists.

In Chapter 4, we propose content and methods for mentoring interns' professional, career, and psychosocial development.

4

Riding Shotgun

Mentoring Administrative Interns

A familiar scene in movie Westerns is the stagecoach pulling into town bringing newcomers from the East. Driving the team of horses were two individuals; one with reins in hand and another "riding shotgun." The person riding shotgun was there to guide and direct, take over the reins if necessary, watch and protect, and provide companionship on an otherwise lonely trip. On the internship part of the administrative journey, mentors serve as guides that ride shotgun. In the case study in Chapter 3, Margaret had two mentors, but only one really rode shotgun. Her second mentor, Sarah Brown, guided her, allowed her to "solo" while remaining there to take over if necessary, protected her, and provided companionship along her journey. During the internship stage, impressions are made, knowledge is acquired, and experience is gained. Mentor-guides help make the journey more successful so that interns can eventually become dynamic school leaders.

In Chapter 2, we introduced five elements of the socialization process: mile markers (time), directions (sources), terrain (content), routes (methods), and destinations (outcomes). In this chapter, we apply these elements to the mentoring process of administrative interns. First, we discuss the elements of time, goals, and sources of mentoring during the internship stage. Next, we discuss the three functions of mentoring identified in Chapter 1—professional, career, and psychosocial development. In connection with these three functions, we discus the specific content and methods of mentoring interns.

Mile Markers

Two mile markers are important in mentoring principal interns. The first is the duration of the internship and the second is the timing of the internship in the career of a principal.

We believe the internship experience should be a full-time, paid experience, preferably lasting an entire school year. Such an arrangement is not always possible, however. Nevertheless, we hope that full-time internships will become the norm as more university preparation programs and school districts understand their value. These experiences expose interns to a full range of responsibilities they might face as practicing assistant principals or principals. Mentoring becomes especially meaningful in this type of internship because solid experiences are available in professional, career, and psychosocial development.

A full-time internship is not an option for some individuals. Many preparation programs have no or minimal requirements for an internship. Because of limited resources, some school districts do not or cannot offer leadership development opportunities. We suggest that aspiring principals seek internships on their own with the help of university faculty. They may consider part-time internships that allow for half-day or part-year experiences, summer experiences in year-round schools, and extended day experiences. The most effective part-time internships are those that have a consistent daily interaction with mentors and a dependable schedule known by school faculty and administrators.

Considerable debate remains as to the best time in a person's career to move into school administration. We suggest two factors that influence the timing of career movement. The first factor is the number of years of experience. The average number of years teaching before entering administration is approximately 10 (Sperry & Crow, 1996). The second factor is the maturity of the individual. Consideration can be given to individuals with less than the desired teaching experience if they have other related experience and are mature individuals.

Destinations

Goals relate to the kind of principal being developed in the internship and are specified in the three functions of mentoring—professional, career, and psychosocial development. We believe principals should develop professionally as dynamic leaders who cultivate learning communities with others in the school. To accomplish this, the mentor models those aspects of knowledge, skills, behaviors, and values that promote dynamic leadership. The mentor also models being a learner and encourages the intern to be a learner. From modeling, the intern begins to understand the complexity of the job and realize that easy answers are not always readily available.

Mentors have a unique role in career development at this stage of the administrative journey. Most principal interns aspire to assistant principal or principal positions within a few years following their preparation program. Mentoring goals in career development are distinct and individual. Each intern is seeking career advancement that will be influenced by the mentoring process.

The psychosocial development goal for interns is not as clear as the other two goals. As interns begin to get a feel for the principalship, role identification and conflict emerge. The goal of mentoring during the internship is to help interns develop methods of dealing with their new roles as they change from previous roles and to help them fit their new role with preexisting roles. In our case study, Margaret's second mentor, Sarah, helped her reflect on how she was balancing the new workload requirements with her family role.

Directions

Although various sources exist for interns' socialization, not all sources act as mentors. Mentors act as guides in some formal or informal role. Earlier, we distinguished between primary and secondary mentors by the amount and degree of involvement in the mentoring relationship. Although the degree of involvement varies, primary mentors are concerned with all three functions—professional, career, and psychosocial development. Secondary mentors are more limited in the amount and degree of involvement but may have a strong influence in one function for a considerable length of time.

The particular sources for mentors of principal interns vary with the internship type and duration. Possible sources of mentors for principal interns are the principal or assistant principal in the internship, a principal or assistant principal in a former school, principals or assistant principals in other schools, university professors, or district office administrators.

Although the building principal is often a desirable primary mentor for the intern, such an arrangement may not always be possible. In fact, an assistant principal often emerges as a primary mentor and the principal takes on a secondary role. Because it is unpredictable who will emerge as a primary mentor, we suggest that all administrators in the district—principals, assistants, and district office personnel working with schools—participate in mentor training. Because the building principal remains an important mentor, matching the intern with the best building principal is important. We discuss matching and training in more depth in Chapter 10.

Mentoring Interns in
Professional Development

Terrain

Professional development includes the knowledge, skills, behaviors, and values of effective and dynamic school leadership. For principal interns, this is on-the-job training. It involves knowing what to do and how to do it in a particular setting. The content of mentoring has both technical and cultural aspects. Technical aspects include learning "how things are done." Cultural aspects are learning "how things are done around here." Both are important for administrative interns to learn to be dynamic school leaders. Learning the technical "how to" but not learning the "how to around here" can hinder interns as they move from one setting to another and as they enter full-time positions.

The case study presented in Chapter 3 illustrates technical and cultural content. Both mentors gave Margaret the opportunity to observe teachers. At King Elementary, Margaret learned that holding a postobservation conference with a teacher had to be done outside regular class time. At Tyler Junior High, Sarah gave Margaret the authority to conduct the conference as she thought best. Margaret learned the technical aspects of teacher observation at both schools, although she learned them with guidance only with Sarah. She also learned that cultural aspects were quite different in the way teachers' conferences were held after the classroom observations.

Routes

Mentors use several routes, or methods, to present content and guide the intern in acquiring knowledge, skills, behaviors, and values. In this section, we discuss those mentoring methods in two broad categories: teaching/coaching and reflective mentoring.

Teaching and Coaching. An important responsibility of the guide is to provide a map and then teach and coach travelers how to read the map and how to navigate certain parts of the journey to make traveling safer and more pleasant. An additional responsibility is to motivate travelers to move faster or work harder and eventually to make their own maps. We suggest these methods for mentors to use in teaching and coaching: planning, informing, suggesting, prompting and challenging, protecting and supporting, and advising and offering feedback.

Planning a course of action for teaching and coaching the principal intern is a necessary first step. One element missing from Margaret's first internship was planning by Ms. Schuker. Without the plan, there was no direction for mentoring and Margaret never fully captured all the learning experiences that she could have with the internship.

Although interns come with ample experience in observing school administrators, most lack a behind-the-scenes view of comprehensive school leadership. They have observed school leadership from different perspectives—student, teacher, and perhaps parent. Seldom have they viewed school leadership from a vantage point within administration. Mentors therefore need to plan a course of action that will give interns these broader experiences.

Inherent in being a novice is not knowing certain things. Mentors should always be aware that a few weeks or months earlier the interns were in classrooms, fulfilling a role quite different from the one they now fulfill. Novices need to know certain technical and cultural aspects of school administration. Mentors should keep in mind that in the next few weeks or months, these same interns could be practicing administrators who are virtually alone and without the mentor's direct assistance.

Mentors, especially early in the internship, may have to tell the intern what things need to be done, how those things are done, and how those things are done around here. We caution, however, that information unloading should be used sparingly. Direct informing does not usually fit the learning style of most adults, especially in a culture that encourages learning by doing. When information giving is necessary, a show-and-tell approach is usually more beneficial.

Tomlinson (1995) stated that the mentor may need to suggest specific possibilities to the intern. Beyond directly telling the intern how to do something, mentors may give suggestions. For example, the mentor may inform the intern about the school's policy regarding fighting on the playground and then suggest approaches to respond to fights. The mentor and the intern can later discuss the approaches and reflect on what worked best, thus teaching the intern to create his or her own maps.

Interns may need to be prompted to learn new things about being a school leader. Prompting involves motivating, challenging, supporting, and prodding. On a journey, our guide may have to prompt us to cross a raging river so we can gain confidence and experience for the next crossing. The guide supports us and is ready to catch us if we fall. Through this method, we learn both independence—how to cross the river ourselves—and interdependence—how to work with others to accomplish the task more efficiently.

Mentors assign interns challenging work, supporting them with needed knowledge, training, and feedback. Challenging work enables the intern to develop competencies and to experience a sense of accomplishment in the administrative role. As interns increase competence and experience, the mentor can gradually increase the scope and difficulty of administrative assignments, again with the needed knowledge, training, and feedback.

When mentors perceive problems in some aspect of the intern's work or leadership style, they should "alert, explain, and challenge"

(Tomlinson, 1995, p. 187)—that is, the mentor alerts the intern to the perceived problem, explains the problem, and then challenges the intern to try new approaches.

Interns learn that they do not always have solutions to all the problems facing school administrators. Mentors prompt and challenge interns to get additional information, to seek out other important players' opinions, and to apply previous experiences. The mentor also prompts and challenges the intern to apply the theory and research from the university preparation program. Without the mentor's support, much of the knowledge learned in course work is soon lost and may never be applied to practice.

A major responsibility of the guide is to be sure travelers are protected. The guide predicts and warns of hazards and harms. The guide also prepares travelers to deal with unexpected nuisances.

The mentor shields the intern from potentially damaging situations and conflicts. Because an intern has yet to learn how to navigate as a school leader, the mentor may need to protect the intern in controversial situations and intervene in situations where the intern is ill equipped to achieve satisfactory resolution. A mentor's decision to intervene and to provide protection is critical in that it enhances or interferes with the intern's learning experience (Kram, 1985). Although an intern can learn a great deal from mistakes, mistakes can be devastating to the intern's morale and interfere with future career goals.

The balancing act mentors play when protecting interns is illustrated by the familiar situation of a teenager learning to drive. The teenager needs support, protection, and freedom. Likewise, the mentor must support the intern's development and determine whether protection or freedom is needed. The mentor needs to assure the intern that support is always available (Odell, 1989).

In the case study, a teacher tested Margaret regarding dress on workdays. Sarah, her mentor, made sure that the teacher recognized that Sarah supported Margaret's decision. Likewise, the soccer dad became so inflamed over the school grading policy that he eventually went to the superintendent. When the superintendent called about the situation, Sarah complimented Margaret's handling of the matter. Not only was she supporting Margaret but she was also displaying Margaret's competence.

Guides on a journey also give advice and feedback to prepare the traveler to take the best routes and to travel more efficiently. Without

advice and feedback, an intern can establish habits that are not con-
ducive to effective and dynamic school leadership. Advice and feedback should be considered in two contexts. First, the mentor provides advice and feedback on the intern's performance. Feedback is
usually provided after the mentor has observed the intern or heard
about the intern's performance. Mentors give feedback to interns
most commonly through informal chats, daily conferences, and written notes. Although informal chats have their drawbacks, they remain a valuable tool for busy mentors.

Mentors also provide feedback on the intern's interpersonal
interaction. Dynamic school leaders use interactions with others to
promote their causes. Their personal visions are developed into collective visions. Mentoring interns to become dynamic school leaders
involves offering constructive and frequent feedback of their interpersonal interactions.

A common mentoring method is for the mentor to plan an activity with the intern, observe the intern, and provide feedback and reflection. Although this simple model is better than doing nothing,
gaps in the process emerge because interns come with different back-
grounds, attitudes, perceptions, and skills. The mentor needs to
teach the skills necessary for the activity in addition to observing and
giving feedback.

Reflective Mentoring. When a guide travels the same route each
day, a journey becomes an act of what Langer (1989) termed "mind-
lessness." The guide has traveled the route so often that conscious
attention is not given to the journey. Mindless mentoring does not
help the mentor or the intern explore the knowledge, skills, behaviors, and values. Mentors are responsible for helping interns make
sense of the journey. Riding shotgun helps mentors reflect on their
assumptions and routine practices.

Mentors facilitate reflection by involving the intern in an active,
open-minded exploration of the mentor's perspectives. The mentor
may ask, for example, "What is your reaction to this?" "What do you
think of this approach?" and "Are there different ways of handling
this?" In the case study, Sarah and Margaret often discussed the district's politics and policies on the way to district meetings by stop-
ping for coffee. Sarah also welcomed Margaret at teacher and parent
conferences. After those conferences, Sarah and Margaret reflected
on what had happened.

Reflective mentoring does not just happen. Mentors must make it happen. Several approaches can facilitate reflection in knowledge, skills, behaviors, and values: writing reflective journals, shadowing, modeling, storytelling, and visioning.

Journal writing is a mentoring method for reflecting. Reflective journals can be initiated by the university preparation program or by the mentor. Interns write and reflect about their internship experiences. Because writing itself is reflective, interns gain further insight into their experiences. Often, without journal writing, interns miss key elements and important issues. With a written account, interns reveal their own thoughts, perceptions, and biases, which can be used in future reflective conversations with the mentor.

The mentor also should write about situations and ideas that are being practiced by the intern. This process allows the mentor to reflect on the intern's progress and to plan mentoring approaches.

Shadowing is another reflective mentoring tool involving observation. Shadowing involves the intern observing the mentor or the mentor observing the intern. An intern shadowing the mentor is usually done early in the internship because it allows the intern to become introduced to the setting, the people, and the culture. Shadowing can also be a useful method of introducing new and different approaches to the intern. The mentor shadowing the intern, however, is often done after the intern is established in the school and is capable of independent activities.

The best type of activities for mentors to observe are those involving the intern's interaction with others, rather than observing the intern in managerial tasks. For example, mentors can observe interns in conferences with teachers, students, and parents and in classroom observations. Interactive activities require the intern to use specific communication skills that demonstrate leadership effectiveness.

When the shadowing activity concludes, the mentor and intern should arrange for a reflective conference. During this conference, the mentor and intern reflect on what they observed. The mentor carries the greater burden in this conference. It is the mentor's responsibility to guide the intern in capturing the key elements and issues in leadership. The following guidelines should help mentors make the reflective conference more effective:

1. Be an active listener. Use good nonverbal cues that show good listening, such as leaning forward, making eye contact, and paraphrasing.

2. Refrain from judgment and offering too much advice. Allow the intern to reflect on options rather than simply suggesting your own opinions.

3. Ask insightful questions. Consider the circumstances and then frame questions around those conditions. These circumstances may change in another situation or setting. Ask the intern to consider those other situations.

4. Brainstorm alternative approaches.

Eventually the reflective conferences can become more informal. As the mentor and intern work together, they engage in a reflective process during the activity. The mentor asks questions as the activity is taking place, which provides on-the-spot reflective practice that helps interns be more reflective about their actions.

Modeling also provides reflective opportunities. This mentoring method is an important learning technique for demonstrating how required activities are to be done, for providing a faster way of learning than that of direct experience, and for learning complex behaviors (Bolton, 1980). Modeling is both a conscious and an unconscious process; mentors may be unaware of the example they are providing for interns.

A mentor should go beyond modeling to prod the intern to reflect on the mentor's activities. Interns may believe that the mentor's approach to leadership is the only approach. The good mentor must combine modeling with reflection, helping the intern become a self-analytical and independent learner.

Part of the adventure of traveling is hearing stories about the journey before, during, and after the experience. Guides tell stories for many reasons, the most important of which is that stories play a significant role in integrating a newcomer into a new culture (Stonehocker, 1992). Guides use stories as warning signals, teaching tools, and examples for reflection. Because the internship cannot possibly include all situations and all elements of dynamic school leadership, reflective storytelling can play an important role.

Storytelling can also be very revealing for a mentor. Mentors may feel at risk when past stories are uncovered. Weaknesses, failings, and mistakes may emerge that can be embarrassing. It is to be hoped that the mentor learned from those situations and can now take the high ground in sharing them with the intern. Storytelling needs to be combined with reflection. Mentors engage interns in reflective activities that help interns probe their feelings, attitudes, and beliefs.

Visioning is not only reflective but also transformational. Through sharing a vision of dynamic school leadership with the intern, the mentor helps the intern develop a sense of awareness. The intern begins to understand the meaning of dynamic school leadership and the possibilities that lie ahead. The mentor sets in motion a new vision of school leadership and supports the intern in believing that he or she can fulfill that vision. Through this reflective process, the intern begins to develop self-confidence for the future and a feeling of self-worth in the present.

Mentoring Interns
in Career Development

Mentoring includes guiding interns to advance to an administrative position. Kram (1985) noted that mentoring for career development is possible because of the mentor's experience, organizational rank, and influence in the organizational context. In career development, the mentor sponsors, exposes, and coaches the intern.

Terrain

Most principal interns will be seeking administrative positions. Their internship includes gaining awareness of how to advance to administration. We suggest three kinds of awareness in career development: career awareness, procedural awareness, and networking awareness.

Career Awareness. Career awareness involves learning the opportunities that exist in educational administration. Most university preparation programs and existing literature focus on three positions in educational administration, namely the principalship, the assistant principalship, and the superintendency. Furthermore, most internship programs place interns in schools working with principals and assistant principals. As "all roads lead to Rome," so all educational roads lead to the building level and therefore the principal.

Educators should focus on teaching and learning as it occurs in schools. Understanding the principalship is important for all educational administration careers, whether they be at the state, regional, district, or school level.

Not all individuals are suited for principalships. Nor is being a principal or assistant principal perceived as being as glamorous as it once was. "The image of administration as a normal extension of the work as a teacher no longer exists. Teachers no longer see administration as a way to improve their salaries, prestige, or respect among other colleagues" (Daresh & Playko, 1992, p. 68). With longer daily hours, longer annual schedules, increased discipline problems, and little difference in salary, many teachers are simply not interested in principalships. Coordinator and director positions in special education, curriculum and instruction, and technology are examples of newer trends in school leadership. Awareness of these types of leadership positions and the qualifications for them are important for interns and for mentors who are guiding interns into a right career fit.

Procedural Awareness. The second area of awareness involves learning the procedures for advancement. Because boards of education appoint school and district administrators, hiring differences exist between districts. Mentors help interns learn application and selection processes. Mentors should inform interns of placement notices, applications, interviewing, assessment activities, resumes, portfolios, letters of recommendation, and other aspects of the selection process in particular districts.

Networking Awareness. The third key content area of career development for interns is learning networking. For a new intern, the mentor serves as an essential link to people in authority positions, such as superintendents, principals, and personnel directors. The mentor helps the intern create and maintain this network.

Networking is closely connected to the socialization process. Interns need to know what people in the organizational culture expect of school leaders. The mentor guides the intern in learning what people in the district, community, and school expect in terms of professional standards, dress, behaviors, and leadership style.

Routes

Interns are guided by mentors through the career development process in three major ways: by sponsoring, exposing, and coaching/advising.

Sponsoring. Kram (1985) defined sponsorship as actively nominating an individual for desirable promotions. Sponsors play an active part in finding developmental or promotional opportunities for protégés and represent the protégé's interests to senior management (Hay, 1995). Hay suggested that the sponsor arrange specific projects for the protégé, both as learning opportunities and as a way to showcase the protégé's talents.

Mentors sponsor administrative interns through written and oral recommendations. Former interns have indicated that oral recommendations were one aspect of sponsorship that they appreciated. For example, one intern reported that the mentor made personal calls to the central office. Another intern said that the mentor had personal communication with the superintendent and personnel director. These interns were appreciative that their mentors personally sponsored them to key district administrators.

Exposing. Interns are prepared for positions of greater responsibility and authority through exposure to available positions and exposure to people who will help promote, develop, or select the intern for those positions. Ferriero (1982) termed mentors "openers of doors." Mentors ride shotgun with interns, exposing them to as many activities and people as possible so that when opportunities arise, the intern will be remembered. The mentor exposes the intern to as many people as possible, in all different settings and levels, who may act as future sponsors.

Mentors also expose interns by the kinds of assignments they delegate to them. Administrative activities that display the intern's skills and knowledge to other administrators and community members can also open doors. The mentor can use such activities as taking the intern to district administrative meetings, assigning the intern to district curriculum teams, having the intern attend interschool events, and having the intern call key district office personnel concerning particular issues.

At times, a mentor may be reluctant to provide exposure for an intern. The risk involved in providing exposure is similar to that in providing sponsorship. It can help or hurt a mentor's credibility if interns are exposed too early and make mistakes.

Coaching and Advising. The role of mentor includes coaching and advising the intern on career opportunities. As coach, the mentor prompts and challenges a reluctant intern. As adviser, the mentor counsels the intern toward some positions and away from others. One former intern described what the mentor did as "interview coaching." The mentor informed the intern of what to expect in the interview process and coached a practice interview.

Mentoring Interns in Psychosocial Development

Terrain

Kram (1985) identified the psychosocial function as that area that affects the individual's relationship with self and with significant others both in and outside the organization. The psychosocial domain of administrative interns involves how interns perceive themselves in the role of leader in the school community and how they perceive their relationships with others in and out of the school.

Psychosocial matters are not often considered in administrative internships. Mentors give more attention to the professional and career development functions. Yet, interns have considerable personal and emotional concerns. These concerns often focus on role expectation and role conflict. Interns have difficulty when they confront the changes the new leadership role has placed on their other roles. They often have to shed the role of teacher, move away from former colleagues, and shift their roles in the family and with friends.

When interns are placed in internships, others perceive them as being both interns and school leaders. The interns are often unaware of others' expectations of their performance in either role. They are also unaware of the authority given them in each of these roles. This produces anxiety that often is dealt with ineffectively by mentors.

A key issue for leaders in a community of learners is the "management of personal change" (Covey, 1990). "Many people experience a . . . fundamental shift in thinking when they suddenly step into a new role" (p. 31). These role changes and paradigm shifts create turbulence in the intern's journey. The usual mode of operation is for interns to handle this turbulence independently, thinking they are strong enough to steer the ship themselves. Interns often look at independence as a strength or sign of maturity. Covey suggested, however, that interdependence is a more mature and advanced concept than is independence. Interdependence is the realization that "you and I working together can accomplish far more" (p. 51). Mentors can help interns learn that interdependence is an essential element in dynamic leaders, especially in their psychosocial development. One of our former interns expressed her need for interdependence in describing her relationship with her mentor: "With an outstanding mentor, an intern can *live* the experience as an administrator and walk in his or her shoes. The shoe didn't always fit just right, but I learned to loosen or tighten the laces as I walked along."

Routes

To understand mentoring methods in the psychosocial domain, we suggest that reflective mentoring involves storytelling, feedback, and delegating.

Storytelling. Storytelling is a favorite activity for school leaders. As mentors tell stories, they also share information about how they handled similar situations. In this way, mentors help interns realize the personal and emotional side of school leadership. Often, interns feel they are the first to experience the role conflicts that emerge and that other leaders and interns have been immune to such conflicts. It is through listening and reflecting on past stories from other leaders that interns develop a sense of meaning and understanding of their different roles.

Giving Feedback. A critical area for mentors is giving feedback to the intern. Feedback can either build or destroy an intern's self-confidence. Constructive feedback produces more positive behaviors than does negative feedback. When offering feedback, mentors should keep the discussion proactive. If interns perceive school leadership situations from a reactive mode, role conflicts can easily emerge.

Delegating. Another important way that mentors influence the intern's psychosocial development is through delegation. Because interns need to see that school leadership involves positive activities, mentors need to delegate assignments beyond student discipline and supervision duties. Disciplining problem kids and supervising halls, parking lots, and lunchrooms produce a stressful job that affects interns' psychosocial well-being. Although interns have to expect their fair share of student discipline and supervision, they need to experience a complete dynamic school leadership role.

Interns often claim that the most difficult period of the internship is the middle stage. At the beginning of the internship, interns are usually excited and enthusiastic. At the end, they have increased hope as they prepare to move on to other challenges. In the middle part of the internship, interns often despair. They find themselves entrenched in routines and difficult situations. Their initial enthusiasm has diminished to a point where they are simply surviving. At this middle point, mentors can renew the internship spirit through different assignments and challenges.

A Look Back and a Look Ahead

Mentoring interns means riding shotgun—guiding interns through the maze of this initial stage of the administrative journey. This guidance serves the three functions of professional, career, and psychosocial development. The relationships between the traveler and guide can help the traveler reach the next step of the journey

In Chapter 5, we move to another stage of the administrative journey. Although not all individuals become assistant principals, it is a common stage. This part of the journey, however, may be a detour or a switchback.

5

Detours and Switchbacks

Socialization and Mentoring of Assistant Principals

Ira: Choosing the Right Road

Ira Smith became assistant principal of Dickson Elementary School in 1995. Dickson was among the oldest elementary schools in Montgomery Township School District. In the early days of the school, Dickson students tended to come from middle-class families, but with changes in housing patterns, students were now more likely to come from lower-working-class families. Along with the changing student population came a dramatic decrease in test scores. The average Dickson teacher had taught in the school for 15 years. Thus, most were accustomed to higher-achieving students and were unsure how to respond to new students' needs. The lower test scores in the past 4 years, along with increases in school violence and drug activity, had resulted in negative publicity, which the school had not known before.

Jack Hess, principal of Dickson for the previous 15 years, had seen the rapid change in the student population. The teachers characterized him as a benign dictator, but one they could tolerate, especially in regard to these new student conduct problems. During the past 3 years, Jack had reassigned one of the physical education teachers as a "facilitator" to focus primarily on student conduct. This facilitator became the disciplinarian of the school, monitoring student behavior, contacting parents of unruly students, and dealing out appropriate in-school suspensions and other punishments. When the school enrollment increased to over 600, Jack requested that a full-time assistant principal be appointed.

Ira and his wife moved to Montgomery Township soon after they finished college. In his sixth year of teaching, Ira was encouraged by his principal, Marcia Reynolds, to enter an administrative preparation program and obtain his administrative certification. Marcia said Ira's commitment to students and to improving instruction was needed in the district. She continued to encourage him throughout his preparation and internship programs and at the first opportunity supported his candidacy to an administrative position. A new superintendent came to Montgomery in 1994 and brought with him a mandate for instructional innovation in the township schools. Marcia praised Ira's strengths to the superintendent on many occasions and introduced the two of them. Soon after, the superintendent assigned Ira to a district curriculum committee and was impressed with his work as committee chair. When the new assistant principalship position at Dickson came up, Marcia encouraged Ira to apply and recommended him to the superintendent. The superintendent nominated Ira and he was appointed by the board with little discussion.

When he first met Jack Hess, Ira realized that Jack was no innovative giant but seemed to be a nice person who wanted the best for Dickson students and faculty. Jack made Ira's entry to the school very pleasant. When he introduced Ira, he praised his work on the district committee and his work with students. He told the teachers that Ira would be filling the role played by the teacher-facilitator. Ira noticed that nothing was said about instructional responsibility and that Jack's focus tended to be on student conduct issues, but he felt he would be able to work with teachers on instructional issues as well. In his early discussions with Jack, Ira mentioned wanting to be a curriculum resource for teachers and talked about creating a staff development plan. Jack seemed interested, if not enthused, and said he was impressed with Jack's energy.

Not long into his job, Ira realized that his role concerning student conduct was enormous. In addition to student discipline, Jack assigned Ira all the special education administrative responsibilities and extracurricular coordination jobs. Also, before long the teachers were sending all their students with behavioral problems to him. Within a month, the line of students waiting to see Ira for some disciplinary problem began at 8:30 and continued for most of the day. When Ira spoke with one of the teachers about why all these problems were being sent to him, the teacher responded that that was how the previous teacher-facilitator had responded to their discipline problems and that the principal supported them in "getting rid of the troublemakers."

When Ira reported that teachers were not handling disciplinary problems on their own, Jack responded that Ira could do his "instructional thing" by keeping the problems out of the teachers' hair. Jack also reassured Ira that with experience he would be able to respond to student misbehavior faster. He encouraged Ira to develop a presence in the hall, in the cafeteria, and on the playground so that students would see him as a strong authority figure.

During the second semester, Ira found that he spent less time with individual behavior problems. He also worked with the new teachers to prevent many classroom management problems before they erupted. The veteran teachers were more hesitant to accept Ira's suggestions on managing their classrooms but no less hesitant to send him unwanted students. In addition, Jack was turning over more community and parental complaints to Ira. When he did this, Jack was always supportive and gave Ira suggestions on how to respond to these complaints.

Ira continued to keep in touch with Marcia by phone and an occasional dinner, asking her advice regarding his role as assistant principal. She eagerly shared suggestions and sensitively listened to his concerns. She also encouraged Ira to expand his role to instructional leadership, especially curriculum development and staff development. Marcia confided that the new superintendent was eager to see what Ira could do with the teachers in using new instructional methods to increase test scores. She reminded him that Jack and two other elementary principals would be retiring in 3 years and that the superintendent wanted to find more energetic and innovative individuals to fill these roles.

As the end of his first year approached, Ira reflected with Marcia on the conflict he felt. On one hand, he knew that Jack had confidence in him in responding to student conduct concerns. He also realized that he had more confidence in himself in these areas and felt good about his work with new teachers on classroom management. At the same time, he realized he had not been able to expand his role as an instructional resource for all teachers. At times, he wondered if he was really cut out to be a principal or if his talents would be more effectively used in continuing to be an assistant principal. Marcia always listened sympathetically to the conflicts he felt, occasionally relating her own stories as an assistant principal working with an autocratic principal. Ira liked the stories because they helped him realize he was not the only assistant principal experiencing these conflicts.

Socialization of New
Assistant Principals

Ira discovered, as other assistant principals have, that the role of assistant principal is probably misnamed. In many instances, it no longer serves as an apprenticeship position for learning to be a principal but has developed its own tasks and responsibilities, focusing primarily on monitoring student conduct.

In hiking, we sometimes have a destination in mind and follow our map directly to it. It is also common that we take a side trail to a different destination, one that seems more suited to our interests or needs, for example, one that is less rocky. This detour bypasses our original destination but leads us to equally welcome sights and places. We also may look at our map and find that moving off the most direct route to our destination, such as the top of the mountain, may be better. We could decide that a route that involves a series of switchbacks is less tiring and eventually helps us reach the top of the mountain while conserving more energy.

The assistant principalship leads to at least two paths: remaining in the assistant principal's role or moving to the principalship. We have chosen to describe these alternatives as detours or switchbacks. The assistant principalship can be depicted as a detour bypassing the path to the principalship where an individual has reached a plateau on the administrative journey. In contrast, the assistant principalship can be depicted as a switchback, heading off in a different direction that eventually leads to a principalship appointment. In both depictions, the tasks may be similar, but the administrative perspective and role socialization differ.

In some instances, especially in rural and elementary settings, individuals may move directly from teaching to the principalship. In urban districts, secondary schools, and large elementary schools, assistant principals are more evident and are often entry-level positions.

In this section, we highlight socialization issues, following our Chapter 2 model, that describe the context in which mentoring assistant principals occurs.

Mile Markers

Mile markers help us decide which route to take. Trail markers that tell us 2.5 miles to a waterfall or 5.0 miles to an overlook help us decide which destination we want. The assistant principalship is a mile marker itself in terms of plateauing or transitioning to the principalship.

The assistant principalship is a period of testing. "As they separate from the old reference group, seek entry and pass through career and organizational boundaries, they undergo a period of testing while the new group checks to see whether the aspirant can conform and adhere to their norms and meet performance expectations" (Marshall, 1985, p. 30). This testing is conducted by at least four groups: administrators, teachers, students, and parents. Administrators evaluate the assistant principal's competency and loyalty. Teachers evaluate the assistant principal's competency, authority, and support. Students and parents assess authority and relationships.

Testing is used not only by the organization and occupation to assess assistant principals' competence, loyalty, and authority; assistant principals use testing to acquire sponsors for career advancement. As assistant principals progress through this period of testing, they take on projects that enhance their visibility with potential sponsors.

Ira's experience illustrates other mile markers of assistant principals' socialization. He brought role expectations fashioned in previous experience that collided with reality once he became an assistant principal. Working as a teacher with Marcia as principal, Ira developed role expectations that emphasized instructional leadership. Other expectations include role features such as autonomy; challenging, interesting work; opportunity to grow and learn new skills; opportunity to make a significant contribution; and work atmosphere (Louis, 1978). As new assistant principals experience the "reality shock" (Hughes, 1959) of the role, the expectations of job control decrease, but the new administrator finds intrinsic job features that are important but largely unknown prior to entry, such as flexibility of schedule (Akerlund, 1988).

Usually coming directly from teaching, assistant principals bring particular expectations of how they will relate to teachers—their reference group for several years. In the beginning, Ira expected the veteran teachers in his school to respond positively to his attempts to be a resource for them. His expectations, however, decreased over time. "The first year administrators seemed to experience a sense of loss regarding their old roles and their previous close relationships with peers" (Akerlund, 1988, p. 181). The process of leaving the teaching role and identifying with the administrative reference group varies among assistant principals, depending on different lengths of teaching experience and different assumptions regarding teacher competence and authority.

Directions

Ira's socialization experiences were influenced by his previous principal, the principal of his new school, teachers in the new school, district administrators, and students. All these served different functions in directing the socialization process.

School administrators are a major source of assistant principals' socialization—probably the most significant source. Principals assign tasks, create role images, and provide support. Austin and Brown (1970), in one of the earliest studies of the assistant principalship, found that the work of these administrators either tends to be assigned by the principal or evolves from school situations. Principals often take the more interesting tasks for themselves and allocate the remainder to the assistant principal (Hess, 1985).

The principal creates a role image for the new assistant principal. In Ira's case, his informal mentor, Marcia, and his on-site mentor, Jack, presented different images of their own roles and different images—expectations—of Ira's role. New administrators "learn very quickly that to be successful in the organization, they must buy into the system, learn the rules, and think like their boss" (Long, 1988, pp. 113-114).

Principals also influence the socialization of new assistant principals by providing support, encouragement, and advice. Akerlund (1988) found that first-year assistant principals most often exchanged work views with coworkers such as principals or other assistant principals, then the school secretary, and finally peers in different buildings.

Teachers are a major socialization source for new assistant principals. In Ira's experience, the veteran teachers reinforced an image of the assistant principalship, supported by the principal, that emphasized student discipline and maintenance of order. They discouraged a more expanded instructional leadership role for Ira.

Austin and Brown (1970) found that teachers and students, more than administrators, tend to see the assistant principal role as important: "The assistant principal held things together. . . . Beneath all the trivia there is a man [*sic*] who makes the school go. He is the one who plugs the gaps wherever they are and sees that things get done" (p. 23).

Teachers influence the relationships and alliances that new assistant principals develop. Marshall (1985) identified this as one of the essential tasks of the assistant principal's enculturation—"separation from and defining relationship with teachers" (p. 45). This becomes a conflict because a positive relationship with teachers is necessary to accomplish student discipline and maintenance of stability. Assistant principals, however, are expected to separate from the teacher group to enforce administrative policies. Yet, some assistant principals affiliate more with teachers than with other administrators, especially if they are redefining their roles in more instructional ways (Marshall, 1985).

District administrators also serve as socialization sources for assistant principals. They develop policies that assistant principals are expected to enforce with teachers and students, thus influencing the quality of relationships within the building. "Frequently policies conflict with local site needs and traditions, meet with resistance, and come with inadequate resources for training, time, or resources for implementing" (Marshall, 1985, p. 46). District expectations require the new assistant principal to learn "the art of the street-level bureaucrat" (Marshall, 1985, p. 46). District administrators also influence assistant principals who want to move to the principalship. Their expectations and assessments of the assistant principal influence advancement.

Because two major tasks of most assistant principals are student discipline and the maintenance of order, students play a significant role in the socialization process. Assistant principals are expected to develop an image with students that emphasizes their authority, for example, a drill sergeant, mother superior, or bully (Reed & Himmler, 1985, p. 76). Expectations and reinforcements for these roles are influenced by students' responses. Although there is little research that identifies how students influence assistant principals' socialization, it is clear that such influence must exist for assistant principals to develop these role images.

Assistant principals are major sources for their own socialization. The type of previous socialization experience and personal characteristics, such as gender, are individual sources of influence. The teaching experience that individuals bring to the role is likely to influence the development of a role conception in regard to student conduct, for example, controlling versus nurturing. The congruence of previous socialization setting with administrative setting, such as social class of students and parents, influences the kind of role conception developed in the assistant principalship.

Gender also influences the socialization process. Marshall (1985) suggested the intriguing idea that gender may affect different images of the assistant principal's disciplinary role. "Perhaps women's socialization and the organizational expectations regarding women's roles enable them to (more easily than men) infuse an element of caring, nonaggression, and support into the task of maintaining control in schools" (Marshall, 1985, p. 53). In addition, women's longer tenure as teachers may influence different conceptions of an instructional role for assistant principals. Perhaps this previous socialization accounts for the fact that women administrators tend to emphasize instructional leadership over managerial aspects of their role (Shakeshaft, 1987).

Terrain

> For the assistant principal—whose daily tasks and roles are ambiguous, whose function is ill-defined, who is caught between students and teachers, school and community, teachers and higher administrators, who are [sic] expected to implement change policies whether or not there are adequate resources— the stress must be multiplied. (Marshall, 1985, p. 56)

Several simultaneous characterizations of the assistant principalship have been identified in the literature, including "hatchet man [*sic*], activity coordinator, handy man [*sic*], and fire fighter" (Reed & Himmler, 1985, p. 59). Such an ambiguous role makes assistant principals' socialization processes bumpy at best. The assistant principal responds by traveling over two types of terrain. We suggest these types reflect a limited versus expanded view of the role.

Limited Terrain. The limited terrain defines the task of the assistant principal in terms of student discipline and maintenance of stability and order (Austin & Brown, 1970; Greenfield, Marshall, & Reed, 1986). Because student conduct is so uncertain, discipline and organizational stability are intertwined in the school context. Three administrative activities are used to maintain school stability: monitoring, supporting, and remediating (Reed & Himmler, 1985). Assistant principals primarily monitor by direct personal observation—being in the halls and the cafeteria, outside the school, and in other places where students congregate and misbehavior is possible. Supporting activities involve engaging students to reinforce exemplary conduct and to accept traditional organizational values. Assistant principals remediate when they attempt to change student behavior to create compliance and conformity.

These activities necessitate both technical and cultural socialization content. Assistant principals must have the technical skills to diagnose and remedy unstable situations; for example, they must know the kinds and sources of information necessary to discover unacceptable and disorderly conduct. Assistant principals must also develop a cultural sensitivity to organizational and community values. What is considered disorderly in one school may be considered innovative instructional practice in another.

Expanded Terrain. The expanded terrain of the assistant principal's role involves a recent view that enlarges the role to support instruction (Greenfield, 1985b; Spady, 1985). This expanded content, without ignoring the disciplinary role, focuses the assistant principal's attention on instructional improvement. Strategies for providing more in-depth instructional supervision usually acknowledge the inability of the principal to accomplish this alone (Glickman, Gordon, & Ross-Gordon, 1995). Because the assistant principal is in at least as good a position, if not a better position, than the principal to assess the student-teacher relationship, such an expanded role would be beneficial to the school. Areas such as improving teacher morale and developing a culture of inquiry and collaboration become important in an expanded view of the assistant principal's role.

In addition to supporting the school's instructional effectiveness, this expanded role also enhances the assistant principal's career socialization. If the individual stays in the assistant principal role, such an expanded view would enrich the role. If the individual moves to the principalship, the role would provide more effective socialization for developing principals as dynamic leaders.

Routes

Socialization routes for the assistant principal tend to be relatively uniform (Akerlund, 1988; Greenfield, 1985d). The socialization process emphasizes trial and error and no clearly defined career path, as new administrators are typically unclear on the promotion criteria. Furthermore, other administrators are the primary socializing agents (serial socialization).

> Divestiture processes regarding movement toward the assistant principal role appear to be gradual and subtle. As the candidate begins to do some of the organizational scut work (that many teachers may refuse to do) associated with monitoring children—helping to "set up" for parent and other meetings, being a "go-for," and helping the administrator with an endless stream of minor (and sometimes major) projects—the "teacher" self is gradually shed and the "administrator" self evolves. (Greenfield, 1985d, pp. 22-23)

Destinations

Ira's dilemma suggests two career goals of socialization: remain an assistant principal or move to the principalship. Continuing in the assistant principalship is influenced by individual preference, confidence, and organizational assessment. Some assistant principals, after getting a firsthand view of administration, never aspire to promotion. They view the assistant principalship as providing the best opportunity for performing those tasks they feel most comfortable and confident in doing. School and district assessment may determine that the individual has skills in a limited area that would be best used by remaining an assistant principal. An assessment that views the assistant principal as excellent in student conduct but poor in community relations could result in plateauing at the assistant level. We suspect that because of the importance of the student conduct issue, some district administrators groom individuals to remain in assistant principal positions.

As assistant principals demonstrate their expertise and sensitivity, administrators groom some for promotion to principalships. More about this goal awaits our discussion in Chapter 6.

In addition to these two career goals, the assistant principal's socialization can have three other goals: conformity, rebellion, and creative individualism (Schein, 1968/1988). Conformity is most likely to be achieved given the typical socialization methods of the assistant principalship (Greenfield, 1985d). The socialization content of a limited view of the role is directly connected with a conformist goal. If assistant principals are primarily responsible—in the limited view—for the maintenance of organizational stability, they are less likely to try to change the content or role (Schein, 1971b).

Because of the typical socialization methods, rebellion is less likely but still possible. For example, Marshall (1985) found some assistant principals who refused to separate from teachers and affiliate with administrators. Such administrators rebel against the traditional administrative perspective. Some assistant principals reject the view of their role as disciplinarian and favor an instructional leadership vision of the role.

Creative individualism is the goal we would expect with an expanded view of the role. In achieving this goal, assistant principals accept the role in terms of student conduct but redefine it in terms of supporting conduct that encourages instructional growth. The values of student growth are upheld, but the means for controlling student behaviors that have little to do with growth are rejected. These assistant principals form relationships with teachers, administrators, students, and parents that build a community of learners to support instructional growth.

The extent to which an individual administrator is willing to innovate depends on their degree of security, acceptance, and centrality (Akerlund, 1988). Clearly, mentors play a critical role in reaching the goal of creative individualism:

Examining the interaction of district preferences, assessment, sponsorship, and support and selection systems may show that people with strong ideals and strong personalities are filtered out of the administrative ranks unless they have continuous mentoring to disguise this tendency; so that they have a defender against those who see them as unpredictable and untrustworthy. (Marshall, 1985, p. 54)

Mentoring New Assistant Principals

Assistant principals and interns travel similar journeys. Most began from the same starting point—teaching. Most are new to the administrative journey and most are new to the countryside they travel (the school culture). Because of these similarities, the mentoring process for new assistant principals has content and methods comparable to the mentoring process for administrative interns.

Assistant principals and interns, however, differ in aspects of their traveling. For example, assistant principals travel with a driver's license, whereas interns travel with a learner's permit. Although new assistant principals in some states and preparation programs have not had an internship experience, their position nevertheless carries with it a contract of services made with the district, which involves more responsibility and risk. Unlike interns, assistant principals are less likely to be forgiven their critical mistakes.

Assistant principals have other distinctive characteristics that affect the mentoring process:

1. New assistant principals have various amounts and kinds of teaching experience that result in narrow versus global perspectives on school leadership. For example, assistant principals have a limited perspective of grade levels and subject areas.

2. New assistant principals come with various amounts of extra-curricular experience. Few of them have had experience in all areas of the school's activity programs and thus they face unmapped territory.

3. New assistant principals have different experiences in student management. Some individuals have not had experience with severe student behavior or at-risk and special education

students. Likewise, new assistant principals have different kinds of student discipline styles.

4. Some new assistant principals come with limited parental contact, whereas others have been extensively involved in team meetings and advisory councils.

5. New assistant principals may have been isolated in their classrooms as teachers, uninvolved with schoolwide programs and detached from building or district administrators.

6. New assistant principals are accustomed to teaching with a structured time schedule and have not had experience creating their own schedules.

7. New assistant principals come from different contexts, including community types and socioeconomic levels.

These distinctive variations of assistant principals' previous experience influence the elements of the mentoring process: mile markers (time), directions (sources), destinations (goals), terrain (content), and routes (methods). In the following sections, we first explore time, sources, and goals of mentoring new assistant principals and then turn to the content and methods used in the mentoring process.

Mile Markers

On a journey, the guide and traveler sometimes encounter road and weather conditions that test their skills. New assistant principals also encounter testing. Although testing occurs in other career stages of the administrative journey, testing new assistant principals affects the mentoring relationship differently from the effects at any other stage. New assistant principals and their mentors feel pressure to succeed.

The testing of assistant principals is a major event for mentors. They often feel pressure because they have invested time and energy in mentoring the assistant principal. Mentors often select, sponsor, and guide assistant principals and are invested in their success. The ability to effectively mentor a newcomer can reflect positively on the mentor.

Directions

In the case study, Ira had two mentors, Jack Hess and Marcia Reynolds. Jack, the principal of the school in which Ira was placed as a new assistant principal, served as a secondary mentor. Jack was mostly involved with Ira's professional development and not so involved in his career and psychosocial development. Therefore, we would consider Jack influential as a mentor but only as a secondary mentor.

Marcia, Ira's principal when he was a teacher, counseled him in making a career move to administration, continued a personal relationship with him during his preparation and internship programs, and sponsored Ira to the superintendent. In his new position, Ira continued to seek her counsel and advice. In these ways, Marcia was a primary mentor for Ira.

Various sources can become mentors for assistant principals. Principals and other assistant principals in the school, principals and assistant principals outside the school, district office administrators, and occasionally teachers emerge as mentors. These sources can be either primary or secondary mentors.

Assistant principal peers can also be a significant source of mentoring, especially for a newcomer who looks for peer relationships. Seldom do assistant principals meet without engaging in a lively discussion about the knowledge, skills, behaviors, and values inherent in their assignments. Peers influence each other by sharing ideas and promoting reflection through modeling and storytelling.

Destinations

The major goal of mentoring is the development of dynamic school leaders who cultivate a learning community. Other goals, however, are important to the assistant principal. Other administrators, teachers, students, and parents expect assistant principals to be competent and knowledgeable administrators almost immediately upon assuming the role. An important goal for assistant principals is to acquire the knowledge, skills, behaviors, and values in a relatively short time. We suggest that it is through mentoring that these can be more quickly learned.

Goals for mentoring assistant principals also include career development. Assistant principals have two future career destinations: remaining as career assistant principals or moving into other administrative positions, such as principalships. We suspect that most assistant principals aspire to become principals. Mentoring directly influences obtaining a principalship position. Without good mentors who assist, sponsor, and promote an assistant principal, a career move to a principalship is unlikely.

Other mentoring goals focus on psychosocial issues. New assistant principals are under personal and external pressure to perform well. They are often assigned the scut work that other administrators do not want. They are expected to handle these assignments under whatever pressures exist, such as balancing the needs of a spouse, children, relatives, friends, and personal interests. Although other administrators have similar role conflicts, the new assistant principal lacks experience and knowledge in balancing these needs. Mentoring is key to enabling the new assistant principal to achieve both the knowledge and the skills necessary to balance the pressures of work and other roles.

In the next section, we apply the mentoring model to assistant principals in terms of content and methods. We suggest that the reader consult Chapter 4 for direction in mentoring assistant principals who have not had an internship or who have had a poor clinical experience.

Mentoring New Assistant Principals in Professional Development

Terrain

The content for mentoring assistant principals varies under at least three conditions. First, the background and experience of the new assistant principal determine what other knowledge, skills, behaviors, and values need to be learned. Second, the role of the assistant principal as defined by the principal or district also needs to be considered. For example, is the new assistant principal involved with discipline and organizational stability or does the role include expanded instructional leadership responsibilities? We maintain that the process of mentoring assistant principals to become dynamic leaders involves the expanded role. Third, mentoring content involves technical and cultural aspects. Technical content involves "how to do it" and cultural content involves "how to do it here."

Mentors should pay special attention to helping assistant principals develop positive relationships with students and parents, which is a common and important part of both expanded and limited roles. These relationships are critical to the assistant principal's role success, especially if the individual expects to move to other administrative roles. Unfortunately, many assistant principals, especially those who deal almost exclusively with discipline, ignore the cognitive and social development of students.

Working with students includes understanding the philosophy of the school, the district, and the community. A mentor should assess gaps in the assistant principal's understanding of and sensitivity to the total context of the student's life. This understanding and sensitivity include both technical content (e.g., safe school policy) and cultural content (e.g., the processes used in maintaining a safe school environment within this community's standards and norms).

Routes

Mentors should consider three methods for mentoring assistant principals: assessment of the new assistant principal's needs; assignment of duties and action planning; and analysis of the tasks, the situation, and the assistant principal's performance. Mentors first assess the events, experiences, and relationships that have socialized the assistant principal thus far. This assessment can occur through a reflective interview and discussion with the individual, through observation, and through feedback from others.

The second mentoring method is assigning administrative duties to assistant principals. In a reflective discussion, the mentor-principal and assistant principal determine the areas in which the assistant principal feels competent and those in which he or she feels the need for assistance. The mentor-principal then provides the resources and guidance for success. Necessary in assigning administrative duties is protecting new assistant principals from duties for which they are not ready.

Not all mentors are in a position to make assignments, but all mentors can help the assistant principal in action planning. Action planning is a process in which the mentor and the protégé reflect on tasks and behaviors that will help in the development process of the assistant principal and the organization. For example, in the case study, Marcia and Ira reflected on a plan of action that involved an instructional leadership role.

The third mentoring method involves the analysis of the assistant principal's actions and the context of the actions. This analysis should be a reflective process in which the mentor and the assistant principal reflect on such questions as, What took place? What should have taken place? What could take place next time? The analysis also considers the context of the action. Different contexts usually determine different kinds of action. Through this reflective analysis, the assistant principal learns that persisting in a course of action, even if it is official policy or procedure, does not always fit the situation.

During this analysis the mentor does not solve problems for the assistant principal. Through reflection and guidance, protégés develop their own solutions. Reflection is the first and most important mentoring method. Reflective mentoring is used to help the protégé learn the ropes and as a decision-making and problem-solving tool.

Two specific methods of reflective mentoring are storytelling and visioning. Storytelling is a common and favorite activity for assistant principals. Mentors can tell their own stories or listen to stories by their protégé. Insiders' stories play a role in the newcomer's integration into the new culture (Brown, 1985). Stories give both the mentor and the assistant principal great opportunities for reflection. As stories are told, information is also shared as to new knowledge, skills, behaviors, and values. The simple telling of and listening to a story can be a developmental process, but when reflection is added the stories become personally meaningful and internalized. Moving from telling stories regarding administrative practice to reflection about that practice takes time and commitment, however.

Looking toward the future is a reflective activity that involves visioning. Often, assistant principals become so caught up in the mundane nature of the job that looking ahead is not a common practice. A mentor wants to focus on visioning often when in reflective discussions with assistant principals. Keeping a focus on the future is a dynamic leadership practice. It affects the way we do things in the school and the need for change.

Assistant principals will be more likely to use reflection if they see it modeled by their mentors. Modeling reflection involves practicing an inquiry approach in the everyday practice of leadership and involves continually and systematically considering what is said and done and then asking why.

Mentoring New Assistant Principals
in Career Development

Terrain and Routes

Although others help define whether assistant principals play limited or expanded roles, new assistant principals also determine which role they will take. Deciding whether to play a limited or an expanded role influences the new assistant principal's career development. This decision also influences how mentors assist the individual in future career opportunities. If mentors believe that assistant principals have no desire to advance or play anything but limited roles, mentors can easily ignore the career development function. All administrators need to take responsibility for their own career development and seek assistance from mentors in the direction and processes of their careers.

The mentor has a difficult position to play in the assistant principal's career development. Because the assistant principalship is a time of testing, others besides the mentor make judgments regarding the individual's performance. This can lead to different opinions regarding the assistant principal's potential for future administrative positions. The mentor has to consider not only whether the assistant principal is ready and willing but whether the mentor's perceptions and those of others are congruent. If these perceptions are not in agreement, then the mentor must consider the accuracy of his or her own perceptions and whether or not to attempt to persuade others to change their perceptions—a possibly risky endeavor.

The assistant principal needs to be aware of what it takes to advance in the profession. A respected primary mentor can be very helpful, but other secondary mentors can also be helpful. An assistant principal should find several mentors for assistance in career development. Mentors should assess an assistant principal's career development needs in several areas, including career awareness, role expansion awareness, procedural awareness, and networking awareness.

New assistant principals often only see one career route—the principalship. This route, however, may be unrealistic and disappointing. The mentor may suggest, counsel, and advise the assistant principal in other career possibilities, such as positions in curriculum, at-risk programs, and occupational programs. The mentor may also assist new assistant principals in considering the possible expanded role of the assistant principalship if they remain in the position.

The assistant principal's career advancement, however, is determined by performance. A mentor needs to help with certain kinds of procedures to display the assistant principal's qualifications. Two procedures that can be used are professional portfolios and networking. Mentors can assist the assistant principal in developing a portfolio that contains a strong resume, key letters of recommendation, and other important elements that reflect the experiences and philosophies of the assistant principal.

Assistant principals need expanded networks of key district and state personnel to further their career development. The exposure that comes through networking makes others aware of the assistant principal's work performance. Because assistant principals can become isolated, mentors need to assist them in maintaining a dynamic network that is emerging and changing.

Mentoring New Assistant Principals in Psychosocial Development

Terrain and Routes

The limited role that assistant principals are often assigned can create a considerable problem. Because many assistant principals have observed other assistant principals in limited roles, they often do not conceive of more expanded roles for themselves. Soon, a sense of the mundane sets in and, as Ira soon found, they are so involved with student management that they seldom have the opportunity for other experiences. This isolation can often lead to burnout conditions that affect the assistant principal's psychosocial well-being.

Awareness of the expanded role for assistant principals is, again, a key responsibility of the mentor. In particular, the mentor-principal should allow the assistant room for personal and professional growth. Every delegated assignment, whether old or new, should include a follow-up reflective interview and conference. Part of each reflective conference should allow for the discussion of personal feelings about the work. The mentor's function is not to be a problem solver but to facilitate the protégé's problem solving.

According to Kram (1985), role modeling is the most frequently reported psychosocial method of mentoring. A mentor's attitudes, values, and behavior provide a model for the assistant principal to emulate. Role modeling is both a conscious and an unconscious method. Mentors may be unaware of the examples they are providing. Reflection on assignments, personal issues, and career concerns brings this role modeling to a conscious level.

Assistant principals may emulate certain features of the mentor's style and reject others. Over time, assistant principals should differentiate themselves from their mentors by incorporating certain features and choosing other unique features. As this process occurs, assistant principals develop a clearer sense of who they are and how they fit into the profession.

A new assistant principal, such as Ira, learns to interact with students, parents, teachers, peers, and superiors by watching mentors— Jack and Marcia—and by identifying which of their interactions are effective. He then models those features of their style he finds effective, perhaps using features from both mentors. Over time, Ira will continue to use some features, discard others, and form his own unique ways of interacting that best fit his personality and style.

Another mentoring method for the psychosocial function is acceptance. Through acceptance, both the mentor and the assistant principal derive a sense of well-being from the positive regard conveyed by the other. As the new assistant principal develops competence, the mentor's acceptance provides support and validation. Similarly, the mentor-principal feels worthwhile when the assistant principal accepts the proffered wisdom and experience.

The assistant principal who experiences acceptance becomes more willing to disagree with the mentor-principal; their relationship tolerates differences. Conformity is more likely when the assistant principal does not experience acceptance. In such instances, assistant principals expend considerable energy trying to please and win acceptance from the mentor-principal and less energy exploring new and better ways to improve. Acceptance is a key mentoring element in developing the dynamic leader.

A Look Back and a Look Ahead

In this chapter, we have examined a part of the administrative journey with unique detours and switchbacks. The socialization context of the assistant principalship is unique in ways that make guidance through these detours and switchbacks necessary and important.

In the next chapter, we move to a major part of the administrative journey that for some is also considered a destination. We examine the socialization context in which new principals learn their jobs.

6

Heading in the Right Direction

Socialization of New Principals

Roberto: From Outsider to Insider

Roberto Ortiz left home early to meet José Garcia at the Broadway Diner—their regular hangout for breakfast and, more important, for talk. Roberto had become principal of East Side High School 6 months earlier. East Side was one of the larger high schools in a metropolitan area of the southern United States. The population of the East Side area was predominately Latino and Catholic. The previous East Side principal retired after 20 years, and the new area superintendent wanted new blood. Although there were two candidates from the East Side area of the district, the superintendent convinced the central superintendent and board to hire Roberto, a well-known Latino assistant principal at a high school in another area of the district.

Roberto was the son of two college professors who had moved around the country. When it was time for Roberto to attend college, he chose a private university in the south, well known for its college of education. When he obtained his teaching credential, Roberto responded to the challenge offered by a principal and the superintendent in an urban school district to help bring innovative teaching ideas to an area that was desperately searching for teachers. At a career-day session, he met José and immediately knew this was the principal with whom he wanted to work. During his 10 years as a teacher, Roberto had enjoyed José's support as a principal and his encouragement to enter administration. After Roberto acquired his administrative credential, he assumed that he would become an assistant principal in a neighboring school. José pressed the area superintendent to go against tradition, however, and hire Roberto as assistant principal in his own school. With a group of teachers, the two administrators developed several nationally known programs, and Roberto and José frequently traveled together to conferences to speak about the school. When the likelihood of finding a principalship in their area did not look promising, José told Roberto about the opening at East Side, in an area across town, and also called the new superintendent for this area, whom he had met at a conference. Roberto was surprised at being appointed to the East Side principalship, since the area typically hired from inside. He was excited about having his own principalship but a little anxious about fitting into a new area, especially one where he was a member of the "right" ethnic group but still a community outsider. Having José close by and willing to help, however, increased his confidence. Roberto and José had arranged to meet each week, whenever possible, at the diner halfway between their schools to discuss issues, primarily those Roberto was facing during his first year as principal. José offered suggestions and counseling whenever Roberto asked for help with problems during the first couple of months at East Side. What Roberto most appreciated was José's willingness to "just listen." As the first year progressed, there was much to listen to as Roberto came to question his decision to become a principal and the toll this was taking on his family.

Mike Jones, Roberto's area superintendent, was excited to have someone with Roberto's reputation in curricular reform. Although he realized he would have to deal with the animosity from two assistant principals in the area who did not get the job, he felt that Roberto's expertise would help win over the other principals. Roberto enjoyed his conversations with Mike, especially hearing Mike's vision of instructional excellence. He had heard that the previous area superintendent had rarely uttered the words "instruction" or "excellence" in the same breath when discussing East Side. Mike came from outside the state and had been given a mandate by the central superintendent and board to reform the area schools. During Roberto's early months on the job, Mike called frequently and gave advice regarding some of Roberto's ideas for reform at East Side.

Roberto's first 6 months as principal were challenging and exciting. He was impressed with the commitment, if not the expertise, of the East Side teachers and found several kindred spirits on instructional innovation. Parents were a different story. Roberto's run-in with parents centered on one major event. When Roberto made his first observation in Coach Manuel Garcia's civics class, he discovered that although Coach Garcia may have had a winning football team, he was not a winning teacher. Coach Garcia, who had grown up and always taught in this community, was well liked by the football team and by the community. He had been coach for 10 years and had had eight winning seasons, going to the state championships four times and winning three of those. The coach's classes consisted of assigning in-class reading and meeting in the back of the room with members of his football team to discuss the next game's plays. Although a few parents complained, the previous principal ignored the complaints. When Roberto met with Coach Garcia and discussed his observation findings, the coach became incensed. He also notified several parents that the new principal was out to get him. At the next parent-teacher meeting, one parent demanded to know why the new principal was trying to "get rid of our Coach Garcia." From the murmur in the audience, Roberto knew this was a hot topic. He managed to temporarily delay the discussion by saying that personnel issues could not be appropriately discussed in public. Roberto knew, however, it would arise again if he decided to take remedial action.

All during his first 6 months, Roberto met regularly with both José and Mike. José encouraged Roberto to project an image in the community that he was there to stay. He told Roberto that if he was to have any impact in the community he would have to demonstrate that he wanted to become an insider. José suggested that Roberto begin attending the local business chamber meetings. He acknowledged that Roberto needed to keep his options open for career moves but also pointed out that this first administrative position was key to Roberto's future career. Roberto was warmly accepted into the business chamber and began the process of meeting several of the community leaders.

At one meeting, Roberto was confronted by the owner of a local clothing store who was the father of one of East Side's football players. The father asked about the rumors that Roberto was trying to get rid of Coach Garcia. Although Roberto assured him that he was not trying to get rid of the coach, the father did not seem reassured.

Most of the teachers were silent on the Coach Garcia issue. Felicia, a veteran teacher Roberto had found to be a kindred spirit on educational reform, spoke to Roberto about the Coach Garcia problem, however. She said she supported Roberto's commitment to making "even the civics class a learning experience for students." She also told him that some of the parents were considering an ad in the local newspaper to support Coach Garcia. Felicia gave Roberto the names of a couple of the more level-headed group leaders and suggested that they might be willing to talk to him.

Roberto and his family also started receiving phone calls at home from parents who were upset about his treatment of Coach Garcia. Some of the phone calls were threatening and insulting and occasionally his children would answer the phone.

During this entire process, Mike supported his new principal, even when some of the other area administrators criticized Roberto. After receiving some calls from angry parents, he advised Roberto to "go easy" on Coach Garcia and wait until the furor died down before preceding with any remedial action.

Roberto called José and asked for one of their morning sessions.

Socialization of New Principals

Although Roberto had been an assistant principal, learning to be a principal involved a new leg of his administrative journey. As Roberto discovered, this leg of the journey is not through the backwoods, away from public view, but "new principals are highly visible and their behavior is scrutinized and open to the public" (Shackelford, 1992, p. 17). Learning to travel this part of the journey and doing so in the right direction are also extremely important for success in later travels. This socialization period can make a lasting imprint and may affect the destination of the administrative journey (Greenfield et al., 1986).

Districts have a stake in this section of the administrative journey. Holcomb (1989) estimated that the average district invests $1.25 million in every new principal hired. Such costs in both dollars and in the teachers and students affected require great attention to new principals' socialization. In this section, we follow the model developed in Chapter 2 and discuss the mile markers, directions, terrain, routes, and destinations of the socialization of new principals.

Mile Markers

As Roberto's experience illustrates, heading in the right direction involves new principals' attempts to become insiders. Although learning to be an insider is part of the administrative journey of interns and assistant principals, it takes on special significance for the new principal. The new principal's ability to dynamically lead demands some acceptance by others in the organization.

Three types of mile markers are significant for new principals learning to be insiders: previous socialization, principal socialization stages, and transitional events signaling insider status. We discuss each of these as they help explain what happens to new principals in learning to be insiders.

Previous Socialization. At the new principal stage, two aspects of previous socialization stand out: prior administrative experience and prior organizational location. Not all new principals have prior administrative experience. The presence or absence of such experience can affect new principals' socialization in terms of the expectations they bring to the principalship, the organizational context in which they are placed, their role conceptions, and individual factors that influence their socialization.

New principals' socialization is affected by the expectations they bring with them and the ensuing reality shock when these expectations collide with actual job demands. If these new principals have had assistant principalship experience, some of the reality shock may be lessened, because they have already encountered the limits of their influence. If the assistant principalship experience was limited to student control, however, information and expectations regarding other aspects of the principalship will be missing.

Prior administrative experience also affects the type of school organization to which principals are first appointed and thus their socialization context. Crow and Pounders (1994), in a study of new urban principals, found that those with assistant principalship experience tended to be appointed to schools with lower staff absences and fewer Chapter 1 (Title I) and special education students. This presents different challenges for the socialization experience of these new principals compared with those without prior administrative experience.

Prior administrative experience may also affect particular individual factors, such as self-efficacy, high growth needs, ability to interpret role-related information, and capacity to respond to ambiguous situations that affect their skills in the socialization process (G. R. Jones, 1983a, 1983b, 1986; London, 1985). If individuals have had prior administrative experience, they may have a more realistic sense of what they can accomplish, how to gather important information for decision making, and how to respond to uncertainties— all critical elements of the socialization process.

In addition to prior administrative experience, new principals' socialization can be affected by their prior organizational location, that is, whether they come from inside or outside the school or district to which they are hired. Roberto's concern with being an outsider to the area and his earlier experience of moving from teacher to assistant principal in the same school illustrate this feature. Prior organizational location can affect such factors as loyalty, reference group, and role conception (Carlson, 1972; Gouldner, 1957). Crow and Pounders (1994), in the study identified previously, found that insiders tend to focus their priorities on maintaining smooth operations and seek their support from internal school constituents. In contrast, outsiders such as Roberto are more external in their outlook, looking to superintendents for support. Prior organizational location becomes an important mile marker for new principals because it can provide differential access to knowledge and experience through which the principal attributes explanations to new events (Crow, 1987; G. R. Jones, 1983b).

New Principal Socialization Stages. Hart (1993), in an extensive review of socialization literature, identified three major stage categories. These three stages tend to involve "periods of learning and uncertainty, gradual adjustment during which outcomes (custodial

or organizational change) begin to emerge, and stabilization"
(pp. 28-29). The first period of learning and uncertainty involves encounter, anticipation, and confrontation and bears the marks of reality shock (Hughes, 1959) and surprise (Louis, 1980a). During the second period, the new principal adjusts to "the work role, the people
with whom she interacts and the culture of the new school" (Hart,
1993, p. 29). As we mentioned before, these issues of task, relationships, and values must be addressed as part of the socialization process. Shackelford (1992) quoted Cabrera and Sours (1989): "The new
principal is like a high school freshman at the first prom—ignorant
of the etiquette and at times a step or two behind the band" (p. 23).

The third period involves stabilization, when the individual
principal settles in or fits in to the new position and setting. New
principals negotiate two sets of relationships simultaneously: one
with superiors, the other with faculty, staff, and students (Hart, 1993,
p. 30; also see Duke, Issacson, Sagor, & Schmuck, 1984). As we discuss in the next section, these individuals become important socialization sources. Other writers have identified similar socialization
stages of new principals (DuBose, 1986; London, 1985; Nelson, 1986;
Peterson, 1986).

Ronkowski and Iannaccone (1989), using Van Gennep's (1909/1960)
rites of passage concepts of separation, transition, and incorporation,
identified three stages that emphasize the cultural transitions of
principal socialization. New principals separate from teaching perspectives and former organizational cultures; process through a
transitional period where they are open to influences from the new
culture; and incorporate the values, norms, and beliefs of the new
culture.

Parkay, Currie, and Rhodes (1992) reported on an extensive
study of new principals in which the researchers identified five socialization stages: survival, control, stability, educational leadership,
and professional actualization. These researchers also demonstrated
that new principals progress from an emphasis on positional power
to personal power.

Transitional Events. Transitional events signal the move from outsider to insider status and act as mile markers to indicate to new
principals their progress on the administrative journey. O'Brien
(1988) found that first task, first public event, first crisis, and first
performance appraisal are used to signal the transition from outsider

to insider status. José, Roberto's mentor, suggested a similar idea when he cautioned Roberto that his first assignment as a principal affected his future career and that the crisis with Coach Garcia was an important socialization event. As new principals work through these crises, they obtain feedback from superiors, colleagues, subordinates, and community members that provides indications of both their competence in the tasks and the degree to which they have been accepted by the new culture.

Directions

The new principal part of the administrative journey is directed by three groups: internal school constituents, external constituents, and the new principal him- or herself. The directions provided by these sources are not always congruent, but all three are critical for the journey. Relationships with people—both internal and external—are critical for accomplishing the tasks of the principalship and for learning how to do the tasks and the nature of the values and norms.

Internal Sources. Teachers are the primary source of influence on new principals (Duke et al., 1984). Not only do they influence principals' tasks but they influence the information new principals have available about their jobs and about the school organization.

Teachers influence new principals by their expectations of the principal's role. Ortiz (1982) argued that teachers expect principals to manage the system so teachers can teach, yet give them a voice in how things are done. Even in shared decision-making reforms, principals are expected to run the school efficiently so that teachers can do their jobs without disruption and interference (Lieberman & Miller, 1991). Teachers also influence principals by being a source of information about the task and the school culture (Long, 1988).

In addition to teachers' influence, other internal school factors direct the new principal's socialization. Hart (1993), using Gecas's (1981) work, identified three factors of the organizational environment that influence principal socialization: "similarity of group members; frequency of interaction or contact among group members; and the tendency of people to interact with people like themselves and limit the frequency and intensity of their contact with people who are different" (Hart, 1993, p. 33). These factors are in part a result of the type of school organization to which the new principal is assigned. Racial composition, for example, can create homogeneous or heterogenous environments in which the new principal is either an insider or an outsider (Crow & Pounders, 1995). Such organizational factors may affect the kinds of information that organizational members are willing to give the new principal as well as the expectations they have for the new principal.

The new principal's predecessor influences the socialization (Hart, 1993). Predecessor's style and behavior can affect the new principal's communication with teachers (Weindling, 1992; Weindling & Earley, 1987). Shackelford (1992) found that "when a new principal arrives on the scene, the school culture responds to everything about that person that is different from the predecessor" (p. 142). This can include gender, race, worldview, and leadership style. The expectations that teachers, staff, parents, and students communicate to the new principal can be formed by their experience with the predecessor.

External Sources. New principals are hired by the district; evaluated by district administrators; and, as Roberto found, accepted or rejected by community members. Although internal sources may have a stronger influence on the new principal's socialization, external sources are by no means powerless. Three major external constituents influence the socialization of new principals: district office administrators, other principals, and the community.

District office administrators, including the superintendent, have a stake in new principals' socialization. In addition to the money invested in the new principal's socialization, district office administrators need principals to enact programs and protect them from community attacks (Lortie, Crow, & Prolman, 1983). They therefore use a variety of socialization methods, including selection, evaluation, and supervision to socialize the new principal (Peterson, 1984). District office administrators also socialize new principals by the way they limit or expand the new principal's autonomy (Crow, 1990; Ortiz, 1982). District administrators can affect the new principal's relationship with important internal constituents through ignoring the uniqueness of the school, pitting the principal against the faculty in implementing district policies, enacting unexpected or uncomfortable policies, or limiting the principal's autonomy (Crow, 1990). Such actions socialize new principals to conceive of their role as being an agent of the district office (Crow, 1987).

Other principals also act as major socializing forces for new principals (Akerlund, 1988). The "sink or swim" socialization (Duke et al., 1984) means most new principals are likely to search for administrators who respond to similar community and district administration demands. Ortiz (1982) found that other principals serve as socializing forces by using humor and oral tradition. Stories about principals who succeeded and those who did not become an important source of information for new principals.

The community also acts as a socializing agent for new principals because the new principal is very visible and open to scrutiny. The importance of this source is evident in the manner in which principals are selected in most districts, that is, "fit with community values" (Baltzell & Dentler, 1983).

The New Principal as a Socializing Agent. A principal looking back over her first-year experience cautions, "Principals should take control of the socialization process, set their vision, refine their reflective skills, and develop the strategic sense needed to dodge the bullets and when to brace for support" (Shackelford, 1992, p. 163). In previous chapters, we identified various individual features that affect socialization. Two features, gender and ethnicity, are especially important at the new principal stage of the administrative journey.

The gender of a new principal affects socialization in various ways, including the selection process, the organizational location of administrative appointment, sources of support, and the content of the role. Several researchers have noted that the selection of female school administrators is different from than of male administrators in ways that affect their socialization (Meskin, 1974; Ortiz, 1982). Because women are discouraged from demonstrating their interest in administration too openly, especially before obtaining tenure, they tend to use their teaching expertise to gain visibility. This affects their insider status and the information they acquire or lack before entering administration.

Gender also affects the type of school to which new principals are appointed and their sources of support. Crow and Pounders (1995) found that new urban female principals tended to be placed in larger schools. The tasks and cultures of these schools may be different and therefore require different types of socialization. These researchers also found that women were more likely than men to mention other principals rather than district administrators as being supportive and encouraging their career development. Men tended to mention district administrators as their sources of support.

Gender also influences the role conception that new principals develop. Research has emphasized the tendency for women administrators to focus on instruction (Gross & Trask, 1976; Shakeshaft, 1987): "Women, then, have been found to view the job of principal or superintendent more as that of a master-teacher or educational leader whereas men often view the job from a managerial-industrial perspective" (Shakeshaft, 1987, p. 173). Crow and Pounders (1995) found that women tend to "view their roles from both managerial and leadership perspectives, emphasizing instructional supervision and promoting caring and respect, as well as insuring safety and maintaining smooth operations" (p. 24).

Ethnicity affects the individual's influence on socialization at the new principal stage. The differences relate to the selection process, organizational location, and role conception. Ortiz (1982) found that the typical way administrators of color reach administration is through special projects, such as bilingual education. This route makes them outsiders to the mainstream by reducing their visibility, limiting their sponsors, and focusing their tasks and learning on more specific rather than general tasks of administration.

Several studies point to the tendency for administrators of color to be appointed to particular types of schools, especially "troubled schools" (Crow & Pounders, 1995; E. H. Jones, 1983; Ortiz, 1982). "Minority principals' schools contain 'hard to teach' students, beginning teachers, and/or teachers who have been unable to move to 'better' schools, and other minority teachers, and poorly maintained buildings. . . . Therefore, minority principals work in inaccessible unpleasant school sites with other minorities" (Ortiz, 1982, p. 104). Ortiz argued that this type of organizational space places socialization burdens on principals of color: They are unnoticed by possible socialization agents and their schools may not provide experiences that allow them to learn mainstream school experiences. Crow and Pounders (1995) found that ethnicity was a major determining factor for new urban principals' placement. New African American principals were placed in schools with high Chapter 1 (Title I) populations, high student poverty, high staff absences, low student attendance, low teacher salaries, and fewer certified teachers. These features affect the organizational climate, socialization sources, and expectations of new principals.

Ethnicity also influences role conceptions that new principals develop, particularly because of the different locations where their socialization occurs. Monteiro (1977) found that principals of color are more likely to emphasize community involvement. Lomotey (1989) found that African American principals are more likely to be committed to the education of African American children. Ortiz (1982) argued that because principals of color are placed in "troubled schools" they are expected "to 'contain' the student unrest and community complaints, but are not readily allowed to make changes regarding the physical plant, personnel, or curriculum" (p. 104).

Although gender and ethnicity are not the only individual factors that affect the individual's influence on the socialization process, they are strong influences. Mentors must acknowledge how gender and ethnicity constrain the socialization process and must be able to expand and strengthen the socialization process.

Terrain

The terrain on which the new principal travels during this part of the administrative journey can be bumpy. This part of the journey has been described as "disruptive" (Shackelford, 1992) in part because of the alienation from teachers, isolation, and uncertainty of expectations.

Looking back on her own socialization to the principalship, Shackelford (1992) identified two general areas of socialization content. First, new principals must change identity and perspective from teacher to administrator. Second, they must acquire cultural and professional knowledge created on the job as they face ill-defined, unique, and changing problems and decide on courses of action. Obviously, those with assistant principalship experience may have already begun the process of changing identity. The specific change, however, is more pronounced at the new principal stage and may have unique qualities depending on the context and superiors' expectations. For example, schools and districts such as Roberto's, which have inculcated particular instructional reform strategies, may expect new principals to retain various teaching norms that reinforce instructional excellence.

In the next two sections, we explore the technical and cultural learning in the two major spheres of the new principal's role: internal and external (Crow et al., 1996).

Internal Roles. Principals spend most of their time in the school relating to teachers, students, and parents. It is not surprising that a great deal of new principals' learning focuses on internal school tasks and involves reinforcing or changing cultural values.

Whether or not they have had prior administrative experience, new principals must learn the names, job responsibilities, sources of information, and unique features of those with whom they work (Fisher, 1986). Weick (1979) argued that work group environments consist of large amounts of chaotic, equivocal information, some of which is selected for use in creating "cause maps" that allow individuals to predict behavior. New principals must also learn the specific cognitive content of their role—the rules, jargon, procedures, and so on (Fisher, 1986). Even if the roles that new principals are called upon to perform are not new, internal school constituents may have unique expectations regarding how a new principal should carry out these roles.

New principals also acquire an understanding of the unique school culture. The specific norms, values, and beliefs that have developed over time in a school are relatively stable elements (Schein, 1992). A new principal arriving on the scene is not likely to change these elements in any significant way (Hart, 1993). Yet, new principals must learn these cultural norms and values, with their tacit rules and assumptions about how principals are expected to perform their roles. They also must develop ways to respond to these cultural elements—either to maintain them or to attempt to change them.

External Roles. New principals not only must learn how to travel within the school but must acquire the knowledge, skills, behaviors, and values to travel within the organizational sphere of the district and community. Early in his journey at East Side, Roberto collided with constituents from this external sphere.

Technically, new principals are learning to play political roles in the district and community. Political skills necessary to respond to environmental demands are frequently overlooked in prior socialization stages (Bolman & Deal, 1991). New principals develop different responses to the demands, especially from district administrators. Crow (1987) found that principals who had moved among several districts were more likely to see themselves as "chief executives of the school" than "agents of district office," which was the view of those who had moved up in the same district. This produced different ways of responding to district demands and affected internal school relationships as well.

Regardless of which perspective a new principal develops, certain tasks must be performed for district administrators, including reports, responding to parent and community concerns, and budgetary responsibilities. Frequently, these involve new knowledge and skills the new principals have to acquire. This technical socialization at the external level occurs simultaneously with developing new technical knowledge and skills necessary at the internal level.

The new principal's learning involves more than knowledge and skills. Districts and communities have cultural norms, values, and beliefs, as Roberto discovered. Schools exist in larger cultural contexts that may have moral, ethical, and political beliefs different from those of the school. Many new principals have encountered conflicts between the cultural norms of faculty and of the larger community regarding appropriate curricular material (Post, 1992).

Impression management is a key part of new principals' learning (Duke, 1987). Learning how to project a positive image of the school and of the principal's work is necessary for the principal's job security and for gaining resources for the school. Superintendents are sensitive to parental and community opinions of schools and their principals notice this sensitivity early.

In addition to the technical and cultural learning necessary for new principals to function in the internal and external spheres, new principals acquire personal learning. They learn to identify their talents and weaknesses and develop a self-image of themselves in this role in this place (Hall, 1987). This self-image also includes the potential role conflicts between work, family, and other significant elements of the new principal's life. Although little attention is paid in the literature to new principals' self-image and these role conflicts, this personal learning nevertheless influences the ways new principals perform their role. Mentors can play a significant role in this psychosocial arena.

Routes

This new principal part of the administrative journey is critical and can affect the rest of the journey, and thus the routes become significant. José, Roberto's mentor, reminds him that the first principalship can affect later career opportunities. In this section, we

discuss routes or methods from two perspectives: general socialization methods based on Van Maanen and Schein's (1979) typology
and other socialization methods specific to cultural learning.

General Socialization Methods. The principal's socialization is individual, informal, random, variable, and serial and involves both
investiture and divestiture (Akerlund, 1988; Greenfield, 1985a). New
principals essentially design their own socialization process with
specifics unique to each principal. Seldom do new principals belong
to a cohort undergoing socialization simultaneously. Their learning
tends to be by trial and error. Even with a mentor, Roberto was surprised by the parental and community reaction he received when
addressing Coach Garcia's teaching difficulties. The steps through
this socialization maze are essentially random; that is, no clearly defined path is apparent and the criteria for evaluation and career rewards are seldom articulated. The new principal gradually under-
stands the criteria that others use in evaluation. Likewise, the time
involved in the socialization process is variable. The primary socialization sources are current administrators (serial socialization). Finally, new principals are socialized through both divestiture and investiture. New principals are expected to leave their old teaching
role and old organizational allegiances. As veteran principals and
district administrators create "us and them" interpretations of conflicts and trouble, new principals receive the clear message that their
old role must be relinquished. Yet, aspects of the old role may be
affirmed. For example, in Roberto's case, his superintendent celebrated his curricular expertise.

Specific Socialization Methods. In addition to these general methods, new principals are socialized in more specific ways that emphasize the cultural learning necessary to perform the role in the school
and district contexts. Shackelford (1992) identified four types of stories that she used to learn the cultural norms and values as a new
principal. Historical stories provided background information about
what happened before the new principal arrived. Organizational
stories provided information about "how things are done around
here." Humorous stories served therapeutic purposes in encountering the sometimes-harsh reality of new expectations and norms. In-
spirational stories provided information and support. These stories
occurred in the teachers' lounge, the playground, the halls, the office,

and the classrooms. Observing in these places, she also gathered information about the school's values and norms. Written artifacts, consisting of organizational documents, memos, and personal correspondence, provided background information about these cultural elements.

Cultural or moral socialization also occurs as principals witness the ceremonies, rites, and rituals of the school (Trice, 1993). Occasions when the entire school assembles are indications of what is considered important. New principals who try to change these ceremonies, rites, and rituals before it is evident that they appreciate them are in for harsh and surprising criticism.

O'Brien (1988) found that novices learned the interpersonal and political aspects of their role through conversational exchanges, school district literature, and nonverbal feedback. Roberto's conversation with one of the veteran teachers, whom he trusted in terms of her commitment to instructional improvement, provided valuable political information regarding parents.

New principals sometimes have the opportunity to hear from their predecessors about school norms and relationships (Hart, 1993; O'Brien, 1988). These accounts help new principals make sense of their roles. Predecessors' accounts, however, are filtered in unique ways that may not coincide with the values and norms the new principals want to encourage. Roberto's predecessor's accounts might have helped in dealing with parental perceptions, but they probably would not have changed his mind on making instructional improvements.

Destinations

We have argued in this chapter that the mile markers, directions, terrain, and routes of this stage of the administrative journey are critical for later parts of the journey (destinations). In this section, we identify some aspects of the destinations to which new principals may be headed.

New principals develop different relationships with internal and external organizational contexts. G. R. Jones (1983b) identified three types of relationships between newcomer and organization. The first, which he labels "naive," occurs when the newcomer is overwhelmed by the entry experiences because of poor past experiences and poor self-efficacy expectations. Newcomers with this type of response tend to avoid interpersonal contact and immerse themselves in the task, thus resulting in perceptions that are at odds with others' perceptions. The second type of relationship is labeled "competent" and involves past experiences that help the newcomer decode organizational content. The distance between the newcomer and the organizational member is less than in the naive relationship, but the newcomer may adopt innovative strategies to create some role distance. The third relationship, labeled "dominant," involves the newcomer who is experienced or who is moving up in the same organization. In this case, the newcomer seeks to resocialize the organizational members by disrupting cultural assumptions.

These types of relationships suggest that the previous socialization, individual characteristics, and organizational response to the new principal may lead to different goals that involve conformity, rebellion, or creative individualism. Many aspects of the organizational context promote a conformist socialization goal. Certainly, the general pattern of socialization methods (Akerlund, 1988; Greenfield, 1985a) advances such a goal. In addition, the specific nature of the school to which the new principal is assigned may encourage more custodial or conformist views. For example, principals placed in "troubled schools," where their time and effort are expended on school safety and maintenance issues, may tend toward more conformist goals (Crow & Pounders, 1996; Ortiz, 1982).

Other combinations of socialization elements may result in the new principal rebelling against the norms and values of the internal or external organizational context. For example, a new principal may respond to the district's socialization in a way that emphasizes alliances with internal school constituents rather than being an "agent of district office" (Crow, 1987).

Innovation as a socialization outcome is possible, however, in situations where both the new principal and the new organization are sensitive to each other and focus on change. Shackelford (1992) described the dialectical nature of such a process: "In order for principals to obtain and maintain their vision for a school culture, the culture must alter norms to fit the vision. In order to fit into the school culture and generate power to lead the culture, principals must alter their vision to accommodate sacred norms of the school culture" (p. 161). The socialization influence of both new principals and organizational contexts is critical to promoting creative individualism.

Hart (1993) argued that often the technical goals of socialization, that is, learning how to perform the job, are emphasized to the exclusion of affective or emotional growth. Attention to the self-image that new principals are developing is a critical aspect of socialization. A new principal who has developed a self-image that lacks confidence and sensitivity to others is unlikely to develop the creative individualism that results in collective visions of school improvement (Crow et al., 1996).

A Look Back and a Look Ahead

We have described the socialization context of a critical section along the administrative journey. New principals travel a varied landscape that has internal and external characteristics that make the learning process unique and open to scrutiny.

In the next chapter, we apply this unique socialization context to the mentoring of new principals.

7

Asking Directions

Mentoring New Principals

Journeys can be full of surprises. They can involve changes in weather, road conditions, and traffic volume. Travelers who learn to drive under one set of conditions, for example, in a small town, but then encounter a different set of conditions, such as driving in a large city, will be surprised and need the special attention of the guide.

Typically, new principals begin their administrative journeys with the desire to become principals but discover that the journey is full of surprises. The perspectives they develop while serving as teachers and assistant principals are limited in preparing them for the journey ahead.

A few school districts recognize this need and have established programs that match a new principal with a mentor principal. Without these mentoring programs, new principals must find their own mentors or stumble along without one, that is, experience sink-or-swim socialization (Duke et al., 1984). In this chapter, we discuss mentoring during the new principal's induction, the "period in a person's career when he or she is in a new position in an organization, under a new role definition" (Daresh & Playko, 1992, p. 19). All first-time principals, regardless of whether or not they have held assistant principal positions, experience a period of induction. In this chapter, we focus on mentoring new principals during the induction period through a discussion of mile markers, directions, and destinations, and then describe the terrain and routes of the three mentoring functions.

Mile Markers

A new principal's induction is not defined by length of time. It does not necessarily conclude after one year and it may take several years (Duke et al., 1984). The length of induction is situational, depending on the new principal's characteristics and the school, district, and community's definition of the role. Characteristics such as those mentioned in the previous chapter (e.g., gender, ethnicity, prior administrative experience, and prior organizational location) affect the length of induction and the content and methods of mentoring. Various school, district, and community characteristics may also limit or expand the induction period. For example, a district or school that is in the middle of dramatic demographic change may expand the induction of new principals because of the increased uncertainty in expectations. Because the personal and organizational influences on induction vary, mentors need to be sensitive to the differences among protégés.

Mile markers during this induction period indicate new principals' progress. In the previous chapter, we identified transitional events that help travelers (new principals) know how they are progressing from outsider to insider. Among these events are first task, first public event, first crisis, and first performance evaluation (O'Brien, 1988). Roberto's first major crisis, the uproar over his assessment of Coach Garcia, was a clear indicator that Roberto had not yet become an insider and had more to learn about the cultural values of the community during his induction. Mentors can guide new principals through these transitional events by helping them assess their performance and celebrate their accomplishments.

Another set of mile markers is created by larger occupational transformations. The principalship has changed since the late 1980s and is likely to be different from what the new principal experienced as a teacher. It involves new and challenging role definitions that go beyond a managerial role involving directing, telling, maintaining, and delegating (Crow et al., 1996). The role has changed from the custodial caretaker to the dynamic leader:

> If there is an all-encompassing challenge for principals in the 1990s, it is to lead the transition from the bureaucratic model of schooling, with its emphasis on minimal levels of education for many, to a post-industrial model, with the goal of educating all youngsters well—while at the same time completely changing the way principals themselves operate. The first challenge, then, is to reorient the principalship from management to leadership, and to do so in ways consistent with the principles of post-industrial organizations. (Beck & Murphy, 1993, p. 190)

The challenge for mentors is to help new principals become aware of these occupational changes and learn how they can alter their own image of the role.

Directions

As at other career levels, mentoring sources are also socialization sources, but not all sources of socialization are mentors. As described in Chapter 6, sources emerge in the internal and external environments. Internal mentors may include teachers, secretaries, or assistant principals. For the first time in their administrative journey, new principals may not have an internal mentor. This contributes to isolation and a feeling of detachment. Although teachers can be very influential with new principals, they often do not have a mentor's perspective. Teachers generally influence ways of performing tasks and understanding the people and the school and community culture. Internal mentors may help in professional development functions but seldom serve as primary mentors to new principals in career and psychosocial development.

External sources are more likely to emerge as the new principal's primary and secondary mentors. Some districts initiate formal or informal mentoring programs for new principals, with veteran principals for mentors. Assuming, however, that a veteran principal is always an effective primary mentor is unrealistic. New principals therefore must seek their own mentors. New principals should not only accept the mentor assigned by the district but also seek out mentors on their own. The pool from which to draw such mentors includes other principals; district office administrators who have served as principals; and, occasionally, predecessors.

District size, location, and culture may constrain a new principal in finding a mentor. Smaller districts have fewer sources, and rural districts often have greater distances between schools and between the district office and the schools. Although proximity is a factor to consider in mentor-protégé matches, modern technology has reduced distances between school principals. Electronic mail, the internet, fax machines, and teleconferences expand communication. Ethnic and social-economic cultures within districts may also constrain mentor and new principal matches. One school may be so unlike another school that a mentor-protégé match may not be beneficial after induction.

Peers, another source of mentoring, have recently received attention in many educational circles. Peer mentors, also known as peer coaches and peer pals, are two or more individuals at the same career level who reflect together on current practice and strategies for improvement, share personal and professional information, and offer each other friendship and support. This type of mentoring has been used with teachers but is relatively new with school leaders. "Given the success and benefits of peer coaching for teachers, it would seem a logical extension to adapt the concept for use by school administrators (Speck & Krovetz, 1996, p. 37).

Mentoring pitfalls, identified in Chapter 1, affect the sources of new principals' mentoring. Mentors often try to clone (Hay, 1995) and constrain innovation (Hart, 1993). Veteran principals, whether appointed by districts or chosen by protégés to be mentors, must exemplify the qualities of dynamic leadership. "Mentors must accept 'another way of doing things,' and avoid the temptation and tendency to tell beginners that the way to do something is 'the way I used to do it'" (Daresh & Playko, 1993, p. 118). Other school leaders, both principals and district office administrators, can be threatened by new principals who have new ideas and approaches to solving problems and creating change. We suggest that mentor matching and training are critical considerations for both the district and the new principal. Matching and training is an area we will discuss further in Chapter 10.

Destinations

From the beginning of this book, we have stressed the goal of mentoring as dynamic leadership that cultivates learning communities. Dynamic leaders embrace change, collaborate in decision making, and foster creativity in teachers and leaders. Although these are goals of the mentoring process, they are also attributes of effective mentors. To establish a mentoring relationship that avoids cloning and constraining innovation, dynamic principals need to be selected as mentors.

Other mentoring goals emerge as we analyze professional, career, and psychosocial development functions of mentoring. In the next section, we identify the content and methods of mentoring new principals, first generally and then specifically to three functions.

Content and Methods of
Mentoring New Principals

During the intern and assistant principal career stages, mentors often repair the road and smooth out the bumps, making sure the traveler is protected and has positive experiences. This is not generally what mentors do with new principals, especially those with prior administrative experience. Sergiovanni (1992) described school principals as leading by hand, heart, and brain. We suggest the same for mentors: a helping hand in guidance and support, a heart for listening and understanding, and a brain for sharing wisdom.

Gehrke (1988), who likened mentoring to gift giving, suggested that mentors give two basic gifts to protégés, wisdom and awakening. Wisdom is a new way of seeing things, a way of thinking and living:

> A transformation results from being given the mentor's gift of wisdom. There is a stirring, a recognition of the import of the gift, of the strength or talent, of the possibilities for one's life—a point where someone sees the potential for genius in you. This the mentor sets in motion for the protégé by both providing a new vision of life and supporting the protégé in believing he/she can fulfill the vision. (p. 191)

Through reflective conversations, the mentor offers the new principal the experience and wisdom that he or she has accumulated. This gift causes an awakening in the new principal and establishes a vision of dynamic leadership. This, of course, cannot occur if the new principal is unwilling or unable to receive this gift of awakening. Protégés are an active part of the mentoring process and must be willing recipients of the mentor's gift.

An illustration of awakening occurred with Jack, a new principal one of us knew. After leaving his assistant principal position and moving to a high school principalship in another district, Jack wanted to set up programs that existed in his previous school. He reasoned that the new high school faculty needed the changes and would be willing to support the new programs. As often happens, faculty members resisted the changes and criticized Jack for cramming things down their throats. Harold, a fellow principal in the district, knew the problems that Jack was facing and invited him to an NBA game. Their relationship grew over a few weeks, and Jack began asking his new colleague, who had been a change agent in his high school for 11 years, about carrying out change in a large high school. Over several conversations, Harold told Jack about the 11 years it had taken him to implement the same changes that Jack wanted to do in one year. Jack always remembered Harold's wisdom, "Think big, start small, go slow." Harold's wisdom helped Jack realize that he needed to move only as fast as the faculty could handle the changes.

Next, we explore the content and methods of the three mentoring functions. In addition to the knowledge, skills, behaviors, and values we have identified in other stages, we discuss important mentoring content such as interpersonal and human relations, political awareness, and vision making, which are especially important for mentoring new principals.

Mentoring New Principals in Professional Development

Terrain

Other than a few orientation sessions, district administrators seldom provide the needed mentoring for new principals (Cohn &

Sweeney, 1992). Furthermore, new principals are often reluctant to ask questions of supervisors, wanting to portray an image of competence and strength. Seldom do they want to risk this image by querying about something they feel they should already know.

In reality, however, new principals face several firsts in their new position. For the first time in their careers, new principals are doing their job in isolation from peers. Also, new principals are now supervisors of others, having formal power and authority given to them by legal policy. Another first is that they now have responsibility for large sums of money, budgets, and accounts. These firsts are unique along the administrative journey.

In a study of beginning principals in Ohio, Daresh (1986) found that new principals were concerned about three areas:

1. Limitations on technical expertise (how to do the job they are supposed to do)
2. Difficulties with socialization to the profession and the individual school system (learning how to do the job in a particular setting)
3. Problems with role clarification (understanding who they are as principals and how they are supposed to use their authority)

New principals in one state were surveyed regarding their preparation for the principalship (Ashby & Maki, 1996). The top 11 skills that these first-year principals believed were important, but for which they felt unprepared, included the following:

1. How to use data to plan for school improvement
2. How to design and implement data-based improvement processes
3. How to use student assessment to gauge progress
4. How to facilitate or conduct group meetings
5. How to make detailed staff development plans
6. How to establish a scheduling program for students and staff
7. How to develop and monitor a building budget
8. How to relate to the school board and central office
9. How to manage food service, custodial, and secretarial staff

10. How to portray a sense of self-confidence on the job
11. How to understand how the principalship changes relationships

Most of these 11 skills are part of the professional development function of mentoring, although the last 2 have definite psychosocial implications. All of the 11 skills have both technical and cultural aspects. For example, the first skill, how to use data to plan for school improvement, requires technical knowledge of analytical methods for understanding data and also requires cultural knowledge of how to facilitate school improvement in the setting.

Several items listed by these first-year principals include not only management skills but dynamic leadership skills. These principals are involved with the change process: how to decide which changes are needed and how to go about making those changes.

Routes

The content areas discussed in the previous section have implications for mentors as they develop the mentoring process for new principals. The first responsibility of the mentor is to assess the content needs for the new principal's professional development. Formal and informal assessments should be conducted early in the induction to identify gaps in professional development. Needs assessment is important because certain management skills are essential for a new principal's induction. If the school is not managed well, new principals cannot implement new programs and processes. Managing the budget is a good example. It is doubtful that the faculty or district administrators will support program and process changes if the budget is not managed well. Furthermore, unlike interns and assistant principals, new principals do not have the luxury of making many mistakes during their induction period. Thus, the mentor's ability to assess needs early determines how much mentoring with other aspects of dynamic leadership can occur later.

After an assessment of the new principal's needs, a mentor should move into other methods of helping the new principal develop professionally. We suggest reflection opportunities that coincide with such activities as storytelling, problem solving, and vision making.

Stories are often told by mentors to share ideas and information and suggest ways of doing things. Storytelling is a mentoring method that is less obtrusive and intrusive than advice giving and suggesting. Storytelling is usually regarded positively by new principals and mentors because it offers opportunities for reflection, conversation, companionship, and collegiality. Without interfering with the principal's autonomy, storytelling alleviates the sense of isolation that mentors and new principals may feel.

Reflection, however, is critical in storytelling. Before they can apply new knowledge, skills, behaviors, and values, new principals need to reflect on their implications. Because a mentor was successful with a certain approach does not mean that the new principal can expect success with the same approach. Reflection gives the new principal an opportunity to discuss the new knowledge, skills, behaviors, and values with the mentor in context. Mentors are key to initiating and prompting reflection. Mentors invite questioning and prompting with such questions as, "What's your first reaction to this? Can you think of other ways I might have tried to do this?" (Tomlinson, 1995).

Problem solving is another valuable part of the new principal's professional development that is important in mentoring. Mentoring new principals to develop problem-solving skills is more than merely finding solutions to help the principal get through a situation. Mentoring for problem solving involves two aspects. First, the mentor needs to teach the new principal problem analysis. Problem analysis is defined by the National Policy Board for Educational Administration (Sweeney et al., 1993) as "Identifying the important elements of a problem situation by analyzing relevant information; framing problems; identifying possible causes; seeking additional needed information; framing and reframing possible solutions; exhibiting conceptual flexibility; assisting others to form reasoned opinions about problems and issues" (p. 3-3). One of the most overlooked aspects of problem solving is involving others in the process. Too often, principals play the role of expert, trying to solve problems themselves. Dynamic school leadership involves collaborative problem solving and teamwork.

The second aspect of mentoring for problem solving involves helping the new principal teach others to solve problems. Too frequently, principals take on the role of being everyone's problem solver as teachers, parents, and students unload problems on them. For example, a teacher takes a student with a discipline problem to the new principal and explains that he does not have time to deal with the student. The teacher believes the principal can solve the problem better and faster—after all, "That's what the principal gets paid to do." The new principal, who wants to be liked and to support teachers, takes on the problem.

The mentor helps relieve this stress by mentoring new principals in ways to develop skills for helping others solve their own problems. Mentors do this in a variety of ways, such as teaching new principals problem analysis so they can in turn teach others, suggesting to new principals a team approach to solving problems, advising new principals to validate the concerns of those involved, and counseling the new principal to follow up with those involved.

Mentors too can be recipients of the "hot potato" problems by taking on too much responsibility in solving protégés' problems. In the internship and assistant principalship, mentors may need to take on responsibility to protect the protégé. Mentoring new principals, however, is different. Mentors must remember where the responsibility for the problem lies and help the new principal learn ways to either solve the problem or help others solve the problem.

Vision building is another mentoring method used to help new principals in their professional development. Vision includes both personal and collective types (Crow et al., 1996). The principal's personal vision involves how teaching and learning are accomplished and includes values, goals, direction, and purpose. "It focuses and energizes the principal's actions and forms the basis for what the principal seeks to influence followers to become and to do" (Crow et al., 1996, p. 78). Dynamic principals have a personal vision that is the heart and passion of their actions. Personal vision also provides the basis for the principal's role in influencing the collective vision. The collective vision is what the school community shares as a vision for the future. Personal and collective visions come together as the principal and the school community attempt to influence each other in constructing the collective vision.

In vision building, mentors model, share ideas for, and prod new principals into developing and communicating personal and collective visions. A new principal's personal vision will never become a collective vision if it is not fully developed and communicated. Likewise, the collective vision will be ineffective if it is not developed and communicated. The mentor needs to model, share ideas for, and prod the new principal in developing and communicating the vision.

Mentoring New Principals in Career Development

Terrain and Routes

Once a principalship is awarded, individuals may feel they have arrived. After all, many who seek principalships never get them. Some satisfaction exists in that one career goal has been achieved with the new assignment and some principals may decide not to advance any further. Other career considerations, however, exist for principals besides advancement. Many principals pursue lateral career movement, that is, keeping the same position but moving from one school to another. Principals consider lateral career movements for various reasons, some of which are location, school size, grade level, community type, socioeconomic status of the school and community, and reputation of the school.

Often new principals are not placed in their school of choice. They seek to move eventually to schools that are more desirable. New principals must take responsibility for their own development rather than relying on the organization. These principals develop their own careers through such activities as university studies and principal association workshops and conferences. Mentors have a responsibility in this process as well. They support and challenge new principals by helping them come to their own conclusions regarding career development.

Supporting and Challenging New Principals in Career Development. Mentors support and challenge new principals in career development in three areas. The first area is establishing career goals and creating a vision of what a new principal wants to become. Levinson et al. (1978) suggested that the mentor support the realization of the new principal's "dream." The dream is the plan (vision) that new principals have for their careers and lives. Too often, new principals travel with their heads down, looking only at the path they are now treading rather than the road ahead. Their engagement in surviving the present does not allow a vision for the future. The mentor supports a protégé's vision, believes he or she can fulfill that vision, and challenges the protégé to work toward fulfilling the vision.

The second area in which mentors support and challenge new principals in career development is through continued learning opportunities. Dynamic leadership involves cultivating a learning community, in which the leader is also a learner. Barth (1997) identified two roadblocks to principals' learning. First, they claim that they do not have the time for their own development; and, second, they believe that by engaging visibly and publicly as learners they will be admitting imperfection. In responding to these roadblocks, Barth argued that principals cannot lead where they are not willing to go. New principals must engage in their own learning and the mentor must challenge them toward that end. To be that kind of mentor, the mentor must also be a learner.

To challenge new principals in career development, the mentor encourages attending workshops and conferences; pursuing further graduate studies; reading books on education and leadership; and participating in principal association, district, and state leadership activities. As mentors role model their own participation in these activities, they encourage the involvement of protégés.

Networking, another career development tool, is important for the promotion and retention of leaders. A colleague of ours became involved in a legal dispute that threatened his status with the local school board. A powerful network of others (parents, teachers, and administrators) came to his support and convinced the board of his innocence. During the court proceedings, the principal was under great stress, which affected his position, his family, and his health. The network of others again came to his aid and virtually picked up the areas that he was unable to handle himself. After his acquittal, he continued as a principal and was honored at his retirement as one of the most influential state school leaders. Such a stellar career could have ended years before if it had not been for the network he developed early in his career.

Network support involves various mentoring methods. Through formal and informal ways, the mentor needs to introduce the new principal to various internal and external constituents. Formal introductions emerge through attendance at meetings, civic affairs, conferences, and workshops. Informal introductions involve social events, sporting and entertainment activities, and service opportunities. Mentors have introduced many new principals to others at golf courses, aerobics classes, churches, concerts, and civic clubs.

Mentoring New Principals in Psychosocial Development

Terrain and Routes

Unique circumstances exist on this leg of the journey that do not emerge at previous legs of the journey, such as authority and responsibility. Although some accomplish adaptation to the new circumstances quickly, other new travelers experience this period with feelings of anxiety, frustration, and insecurity. As travelers learn the rules of this leg of the journey, they also learn an understanding of their role and its relationship to others' roles.

Because achieving independence and being able to "run the ship" equate to achieving equal status with colleagues, school principals frequently do not seek direct help from others. Often, independence hides principals' psychosocial concerns and discourages them from obtaining professional advice. New principals face many challenges in their psychosocial development, two of which are isolation and role ambivalence.

Alone and Lost in the Forest: Isolation and Environment. New travelers on a strange road need to keep their heads up to see what lies ahead, and they need to look back to see who is there. At times, when they look back, they find themselves alone in the forest with no one following them and no understanding of how to get out. The further the traveler goes into the forest, the lonelier and darker it becomes. Soon, the traveler becomes hopelessly lost and can only call out for help to anyone in listening distance who might be willing to help.

A critical area for new principals is that they find themselves very much alone. Although some new principals choose to isolate themselves, environment also causes isolation in at least four ways. First, new principals are no longer teachers and are not yet accepted in the administrative ranks. Second, many schools still follow industrial models of labor and management in which teachers are on one side of the fence and administrators are on the other side. Third, the hectic schedule of principals often inhibits interaction with others. Fourth, new principals often feel they need to follow the rules, policies, and procedures down to crossing each "t" and dotting each "i." The more new principals isolate themselves from others, the more isolated they become. Isolation begets isolation.

Building Bridges: Mentoring to Avoid and Reduce Isolation. Mentors can help new principals avoid and reduce isolation. One mentoring method is helping the new principal build bridges with internal and external constituents. A new principal can connect with internal constituents by being visible, available, and approachable. The mentor, however, must help the new principal realize that not all internal constituents are willing to connect. Rejection is a hard lesson for some new principals.

Building bridges with external constituents is akin to collegial networking in that new principals connect with peers outside the school. The mentor becomes a key individual to help build bridges in the external environment.

Frequently, the new principal needs nothing more than a sounding board. Often, the new principal feels isolated and only wants a sympathetic ear and a caring response, with no advice or solution given. Mentors can be great listeners but can also be advice givers. Because many new principals seek autonomy, giving advice at this career stage is usually not an effective mentoring approach.

Driving Through Fog: Role Ambiguity. On a journey, travelers may encounter fog that clouds the terrain and causes them to become confused and disoriented. They once again look for help from their guides.

Most new principals know they have been given much responsibility, faced as they are with managing and supervising faculty and staff, programs, and resources that affect young people's lives. With this responsibility, they are surprised to learn how little control they often have. They learn they are responsible for everything in the building and everyone expects them to "make it right." Hart and Bredeson (1996) wrote that responsibility without control creates role ambiguity and role anxiety for principals. Role ambiguity can be seen almost daily in the principal's office. Principals have to deal with problems they did not cause, make decisions without enough information, and fix things that are not theirs to fix. New principals can become so confused with this new role that they become indecisive and apprehensive, resulting in feelings of incompetence and helplessness.

Encountering the Familiar: Mentoring to Reduce Role Ambiguity. Driving out of the fog, travelers encounter familiar terrain, signs, and other landmarks that change their anxiety to relief. Mentors can help protégés relieve their anxiety by finding a comfort zone. Drawing on their past successes and experiences, most new principals find solutions to new problems. With the feeling of being at home, new principals find prominence, clarity, certainty, and assurance. These things can lead the new principal to find less role ambiguity.

A Look Back and a Look Ahead

Mentoring new principals involves unique features due to the nature of this leg of the administrative journey. We have discussed the unique content and methods of mentoring new principals.

In the next chapter, we travel to the final leg of our journey—mid-career. This leg of the journey is frequently ignored by both practitioners and those who could be mentors to them. Yet, it is a critical part of the journey if we want dynamic leaders who have the clout and experience to create learning communities.

8

Refueling

Socialization of
Mid-Career Administrators

Norma: Changing Routes and Refueling

After the last teacher in the building stopped by to wish her a good summer vacation, Norma Ginsburg sat at her desk pondering the year that just ended. In her 10th year of administration, Norma thought things were supposed to calm down, but this year had been a year of changes. She had moved from Krouch Elementary in a neighboring district to Dayton Elementary in Brunswick Unified School District. And she had been elected president of the state elementary principals' association. She had told her friend Sue Kowalski, a fellow principal in the previous district, that this was the last set of changes like this she could handle.

Norma decided to leave Krouch Elementary not because she was dissatisfied. In fact, she had developed a great relationship with the teachers, students, and parents over the 10 years at Krouch. She had decided she needed a change. Her youngest child was off to college and her husband's job was demanding more and more travel. She explored several openings in her own district and even toyed with the idea of applying for a superintendency. When the superintendent of the Brunswick district described the situation at Dayton Elementary, she decided this might be the challenge she wanted.

Dayton Elementary School had once been among the few Schools of Excellence in the state. It was an early site-based managed school and had a reputation for innovative instructional practices. With a change in demographics to a more heterogeneous student population, teachers had grown weary of the constant reforms and increasing time demands. Most of the best teachers had long since left. The remaining teachers, who were unable to leave because of their personal situations or because they were not marketable, had become bitter and even belligerent toward the former principal. Several teachers were under remediation in the teacher evaluation process. The superintendent told Norma that she would be willing to back Norma's efforts to revitalize the staff and to infuse the school with new resources to bring back the school's earlier innovative culture.

Before making the decision to move, Norma had long conversations with her friend Sue. The two had taught together in the same school and been in the same cohort in an administrator preparation program. When they both were appointed to schools in the same district, they met together every Monday evening for dinner to talk about problems they encountered and share stories. They helped each other through some difficult times. Norma held Sue's hand during a rough teacher grievance situation when the union tried to get Sue fired. Sue also helped Norma through her divorce from her first husband. She was the one who nominated Norma for the presidency of the principals' association. Sue had held the position 2 years earlier and had asked Norma to chair the spring conference. During this time, the two were frequently referred to as Thelma and Louise. They often laughed about the similarities.

Norma told Sue that although she enjoyed her work at Krouch Elementary, she always wondered if she could succeed as a principal in a more troubled environment. Since Norma had once taught at Krouch, she questioned if her success was at least partly due to her earlier association with the school. Norma always appreciated Sue's willingness to listen and her candor, especially when Norma got into her "down state." Sue encouraged Norma to stop wondering and start testing the waters. She also wrote a letter of recommendation for Norma to the superintendent in the Brunswick district.

Soon after her appointment to the Dayton school, Norma realized that her leadership style at Krouch Elementary might need to be altered at Dayton. She was accustomed to working with teachers in developing collective visions for both the school and individual classrooms. Even the Krouch teachers who were having problems responded well to her facilitative and indirect style. She was able to sit with teachers and encourage them to solve classroom problems. Teachers praised the way she asked such great questions that encouraged them to identify problems and settle on solutions themselves.

She soon learned that Dayton teachers did not respond positively to her indirect style. When she tried to use her previous style in working with those having instructional problems, they either sat in stony silence or accused her of manipulating them. One teacher shouted at her, "Just tell me what you want me to do!"

She also realized that ample documentation existed to request termination of at least two teachers. When she observed their classes, they did little to impress her or to suggest that they were trying to improve. The two teachers gave out worksheets and responded sarcastically to the few questions that students raised. Soon after her appointment, several parents pleaded to have their children placed with other teachers.

During this early period, Martha, a friend of Norma's from college and a veteran teacher at the school, frequently stopped by to encourage Norma. She and Norma had known each other for years, and, in fact, Martha had called Norma to tell her about the Dayton job and beg her to apply. As Norma soon discovered, Martha was one of the few good teachers who had remained at the Dayton school. Martha's aging mother lived in the area and Martha did not want to change schools. "Besides," she told Norma, "I have a commitment to the children of this community. I don't want to give up on them."

Soon after Norma had observed the teachers under remediation, she and Martha went out for coffee after school. Martha encouraged Norma to proceed with the termination of these teachers. She said that several teachers at the school were potentially good teachers but were weary of past administrators' unwillingness to get rid of poor teachers. They wondered why they should put in long hours, attend professional development sessions, and agree to new innovative techniques when these poor teachers could still earn a paycheck. Martha encouraged Norma to take a more directive style, at least in the beginning, so that teachers would see that she meant business and was willing to make hard decisions.

Norma confided in Martha that this more directive style was uncomfortable for her and she felt uneasy beginning with one style and then switching. Martha encouraged her to think developmentally about the school and her leadership style. If she wanted teachers to eventually respond to a more indirect, facilitative style, she was going to have to make difficult decisions now and be more directive with those teachers who were not responding to her. Norma appreciated Martha's candor and support, but she was not sure changing her style would work. Would the teachers not see it as arbitrary or artificial or worse?

In the midst of the trouble in the school, Norma encountered a minor but potentially major conflict in the board of the principals' association. Some of the urban principals felt that the association had spent too much time in the past 3 years discussing rural issues and not enough attention was being paid to urban problems. Norma acknowledged that rural school issues were the main themes at the last association conference and at two other workshops. She reminded the board that for years no attention was paid to rural issues in the association. After one tense board meeting, Norma sat with Sue. The conflict perplexed her and she could not understand why these board members were so upset. Sue suggested that these individuals might be trying to make themselves more visible in order to run for president at the next election. She told Norma that the rural/urban conflict on the board resurfaced every now and then, but this time it might have more to do with the personalities and aspirations of a few individuals than any widespread discontent. Sue gave Norma the name of an old-timer in the association who also knew the individuals in question.

As Norma sat at her desk, she wondered what next year would bring. Would she be reelected for a second term as association president and did she even want to be reelected? Would she be able to change her style to respond to the internal conflicts at Dayton school and did she really want to?

The Socialization of Mid-Career Administrators

Norma's socialization at this mid-career point of her administrative journey is different from the socialization of interns, new assistant principals, and new principals. Before we address elements of the mid-career stage of the administrative journey, we define mid-career, discuss its importance for school reform, and identify some unique features of this stage of the journey.

Definition of Mid-Career

Mid-career is a confusing concept. It does not necessarily occur at the middle point of an administrative career. Hall, a leading theorist in mid-career socialization, defined this period as occurring "during one's work in an occupational (career) role after one feels established and has achieved perceived mastery and prior to the commencement of the disengagement process" (1986, p. 127). Mid-career is determined more by the individual's perception than by the number of years in a career role. It occurs after individuals perceive they have mastered the role's basic knowledge, skills, behaviors, and values and before they begin to move toward retirement or termination of their role involvement. For administrators, mid-career can occur after they perceive they have survived the initial reality shock of the assistant principal or principal role and adjusted to the demands and expectations. Survival can last a few months or a few years (Parkay et al., 1992).

"Resocialization becomes necessary when an experienced manager changes jobs, is promoted, transfers to another department, or changes companies. The extent to which such changes require readjustment depends on how different the new position is from the former position" (London, 1985, p. 24). Norma's case illustrates three major mid-career transitions. First, she moved to a different school. Second, she faced the need to change her image of the principal's role. Third, she took on an extra role with her election as state elementary principals' association president.

Mid-Career Socialization as Critical for School Reform. Literature on school reform has tended to emphasize the preparation of new school administrators (Griffiths et al., 1988). Two reasons exist for this emphasis. First, reforms, such as clinical field experiences, have centered on schools of education that prepare administrators. Second, the research on socialization has emphasized entry-level processes. "The central assumption of this research on role transitions has been a tilted power relationship, with a low-power individual moving into a high-power work environment, with a resulting one-way influence process. The organization socializes the person, but the person does not innovate or otherwise act on the organization" (Hall, 1986, p. 121).

"Restructuring schools means reconceptualizing roles" (Crow, 1993, p. 131). Because more mid-career administrators exist than new administrators, these individuals are in a better position to make a difference in schools' cultural values and beliefs. Understanding how veteran, or mid-career, administrators learn new roles or new role conceptions is critical for understanding how reform is possible.

Unique Features of Mid-Career Socialization. Although Norma's socialization involving school change, role conceptions, and extra roles has similarities to earlier socialization experiences, these experiences are unique in several respects. Hall (1980, 1986) identified the unique elements of mid-career experiences that are useful to our understanding. Among these elements are the following:

- Fewer institutionalized status passages
- More often an individual process than a collective one
- More a process of individuation than socialization
- Nonwork, family status passages become more important
- Heightened sense of career ambiguity
- Heightened awareness of longer-term dimensions of career effectiveness
- Partially a process of undoing earlier career socialization
- Different sources of influence
- Increased salience of separating from old role

These elements will be illustrated as we discuss the mile markers, directions, terrain, routes, and destinations of mid-career socialization. Mid-career socialization is not the same as entry-level socialization and therefore the content and methods of mentoring are different at this stage of the administrative journey.

Mile Markers

Norma's mid-career administrative journey involved several mile markers. She changed schools, added an extra role, and struggled with changing her role conception. In addition, various stages, including exploration and trial, were marked in her journey. Norma's experience illustrates two types of mile markers: role transitions and stages of mid-career socialization.

Role Transitions. We have already identified three types of transition that Norma experienced. These are classified in the literature as interrole and intrarole transitions (Louis, 1980b). Work transitions are "any major change in work role requirements or work context" (Nicholson & West, 1989, p. 182). This definition emphasizes that a variety of transitions can occur during the career that necessitate new learning. Louis's (1980b) typology of work role transitions included the following:

- Interrole transitions: Entry/reentry; Intracompany; Intercompany; Interprofession; Exit
- Intrarole transitions: Intrarole adjustment; Extrarole adjustment; Role/career stage transition; Life stage transition

The most obvious transitions for mid-career administrators are interrole transitions involving changing schools (intercompany transition) and changing positions within the district (intracompany transition). The most frequent intrarole transitions are changing role conceptions (intrarole adjustment); adding an additional role, such as leadership in a professional association (extrarole adjustment); moving from survival to mastery (career stage transition); and moving to a new family stage, for example, empty nest (life stage transition).

Any transition involves new learning to understand how to perform the role in a different setting, different job, additional role, or changed role. If the features of the new role are dramatically different from the old role, the administrators have more coping to do. Thus, the socialization process should be more complex than if the change involves little contrast, for example, only slightly altering the role image.

Mid-Career Stages. The mid-career portion of the administrative journey is also marked by various stages in the necessary transitions. These stages are similar in some respects to those we identified in earlier parts of the administrative journey, such as encounter, adjustment, and stabilization (Hart, 1993). Nicholson and West (1989;

Nicholson, 1987), for example, identified five stages: (a) preparation (expectation and anticipation before change), (b) encounter (affect and sense making during the first days or weeks of job tenure), (c) adjustment (subsequent personal and role development to reduce person-job misfit), (d) stabilization (settled connection between person and role), and (e) preparation (renewal of the cycle). The model differs from earlier career stage models by acknowledging the cyclical nature of the process, that is, an ongoing quality to adjustment rather than completion. This suggests the continual nature of mid-career changes. The model also admits the possibility of role making in which the individual fits the job to the self instead of the self to the job (Mead, 1934). Role making is especially relevant in mid-career when the individual brings a repertoire of previous skills, knowledge, and values to the transition and has already developed a role identity.

Some theorists have argued that the likelihood of personal change (fitting the self to the job) is greater at early stages of the career, for example, at entry, and that role change (fitting the job to the self) is more likely to occur at mid-career stages (Katz, 1980; Schein, 1971a). This argument assumes that individuals bring an identity with them into the mid-career change. Nicholson (1984) challenged this argument with his research on managers that showed that role and personal development seem to occur together rather than separately. He found that role development tends to be a strong and continual response to work from the beginning; managers hit the ground running. He also found that personal development takes longer, is slower, and is harder to detect. We argue that although new administrators are likely to do some fitting of the job to self, the degree of role development is likely to be less than at mid-career since mid-career administrators already possess basic knowledge, skills, behaviors, and values that new principals lack.

Other stage models suggest unique qualities of mid-career change. Hall's (1986) learning cycle emphasized the exploration quality of mid-career transitions. The cycle begins with a heightened awareness of choice, when "career routines" have been disrupted, for example, when an individual's earlier role and organizational satisfaction decrease. Following this, the individual begins to explore options that might be more in line with his or her values, interests, skills, satisfactions, and relationships. Next, the individual progresses through a trial period. For example, administrators who are exploring new role images might agree to serve on a district committee or task force discussing new governance structures for schools (Crow, 1993). After this trial period, the individual makes a personal choice, which could mean either staying or leaving the current role, organization, or conception. Following this choice is a period of "subidentity transition" in which the individual leaves the old role; learns new skills, knowledge, and attitudes; and modifies self-concept. Over time, the individual becomes established in the new role, incorporating the new subidentity into the total identity and meshing it with past identity (Hall, 1986). The two final parts of the cycle involve a heightened level of adaptability and a heightened awareness of self as career agent. These two result from the process of exploring, trying on new roles, and making choices and involve the realization by individuals that they can adapt to new situations. This realization causes individuals to acknowledge the power they have as agents of their own careers. Thus, a mid-career administrator who has once made a career change (e.g., moved to another school) may be more likely to positively consider other transitions (e.g., adjusting the role image).

Directions

Norma's mid-career administrative journey was guided by several sources, including the old and new schools, the district office, professional associations, her family, and herself. In this section, we first discuss general socialization sources unique to mid-career stages. We then move to a presentation of the more specific sources for mid-career administrators' socialization.

General Sources of Mid-Career Socialization. Three major categories of mid-career sources that disrupt career routines are organizational or societal sources, work role sources, and personal sources (Hall, 1986). Organizational sources of mid-career socialization include major changes in the job or organization that call for significantly different work skills. These involve changes in technology and economic fluctuations. They also involve organizational characteristics such as a climate that encourages or discourages growth and rewards or sanctions change.

Work role sources involve the nature of the job, that is, whether or not variety and mastery increase. Other sources, such as role models and mentors as well as the relationships that form in the work environment, influence mid-career socialization.

Finally, personal sources can trigger mid-career change and socialization. Changes in family, personal health, age, personal insight, and personality characteristics can help disrupt career routines and begin the socialization process. The role of self in mid-career transition is critical. Throughout this book, we have maintained that socialization processes are not passive, and individuals have an active role to play. Nowhere is this more vivid and active than at mid-career. The self as a mid-career socialization source acts in two ways: as a trigger for change and as an influence on the socialization process. Changes in the individual's values, interests, needs, or skills, brought on by changes in life and family stage, organizational environment, or work role requirements, can trigger exploration, trial, and choice in mid-career transition (Hall, 1980, 1986). In Norma's case, her children leaving home and her desire for a new challenge led her to explore new career options.

As we have noted earlier, role development, or fitting the role to the self, emphasizes the active part that the individual plays. Instead of simply accepting the role as given by the organization, the individual at mid-career actively molds the job to fit the self.

Several individual qualities influence the socialization process. Personality characteristics, such as flexibility, tolerance for ambiguity and uncertainty, hardiness, and motivational orientation affect the way mid-career individuals explore, try on, choose, and incorporate the new role (Hall, 1986; Nicholson, 1984). In addition, prior occupational socialization influences the mid-career process (Nicholson, 1984). At mid-career, the influence of an individual's prior socialization is heightened and should have more influence on the personal and role development goals that are achieved.

Mid-Career Administrator Socialization Sources. Various societal, organizational, work role, and personal elements can trigger mid-career changes and the socialization process for administrators. Current societal preoccupation with models of leadership that emphasize shared decision making influence the ways school administrators view their role (Crow, 1993). Organizational reforms that create demands for reconceptualizing the administrator's role to a more facilitative style also influence mid-career change. The changing student demographics, technology changes, and other factors that affect the way the work is performed influence mid-career change. The era of stable and consistent administrators' roles has passed.

In addition to these societal, organizational, and work role factors that trigger the disruption of career routines at this stage, other sources influence the socialization process. District administrators remain a major force affecting mid-career socialization. Peterson (1987) identified how districts use careers to "develop skills, foster the internalization of values, mold beliefs and norms of behavior, promote the development of internal organizational communication networks, and reinforce a reward system based on promotion" (p. 4). Although this influence begins at entry, districts continue to influence school administrators throughout their careers.

Internal school constituents also influence the mid-career socialization process, as Norma discovered. When mid-career administrators enter a new school or change their role conceptions, they encounter teachers, parents, and students with predetermined expectations of how a new administrator will behave, even if that administrator is a veteran. As one principal who decided to move to another school heard from a teacher, "We just got you trained." Furthermore, as we mentioned in Chapter 6, predecessors influence the socialization process (Hart, 1993). Although mid-career administrators are not novices to the role, the expectations of teachers, students, and parents of the mid-career administrator are influenced by the style, personality, and relationships of the predecessor.

In addition to the larger societal, district, and school influences on the mid-career administrator's socialization, the individual administrator takes an active part in the socialization process. As Hall (1980) and others found, at mid-career individuals are more likely to be their own socialization agents, exploring alternative career moves, trying on new role images, and developing a subidentity that meshes with past identity. If mid-career administrators are fortunate, they have mentors to help with this exploration. The administrator's prior socialization affects this exploration and trial process. Crow (1987) found that principals who had moved between several districts had a greater opportunity to witness alternative responses to district office/school relationship problems than principals whose career had been restricted to one district. Thus, prior socialization restricts or expands the exploration process in which alternative role conceptions are considered.

Families and friends also influence mid-career administrators. Family and life stage changes influence the favorableness of options, the process of leaving an old role, and the developing identity that is incorporated into the new role or image.

Terrain

The terrain of the mid-career administrative journey depends on the kind of transition. If the administrator changes schools, as Norma did, the terrain involves a new set of skills and values. The terrain also involves new knowledge (information regarding group dynamics) and new skills (how to share decision making) if the administrator changes role conceptions. If the administrator's career stage changes, the terrain involves new dispositions regarding the balance of work and personal life.

The differences between old role and new role influence socialization content. Little attention has been paid to the process of leaving an old role (Louis, 1980a). At mid-career, leaving the old role is a critical feature of the process. If the knowledge, skills, behaviors, and values of the new role are dramatically different from those of the old role, the socialization content is a major issue. Frequently, the change from old role to new is not "socially celebrated" (Louis, 1980a), that is, the process is more gradual than dramatic. Hughes (1959) described the physician who over time takes on more administrative responsibility and less direct, clinical involvement with patients. The role conception has changed but not in a dramatic, socially acknowledged way.

A unique feature of mid-career change is the heightened awareness of two longer-term dimensions of career effectiveness (Hall, 1986). Instead of performance and attitude, which are emphasized at early career stages, identity and adaptability to outcomes are more pronounced at mid-career. Content involved in the following questions becomes critical: "What do I want to do with the rest of my life? How can I make the changes necessary to remain on top in my field or to move into a new field?" (Hall, 1986, p. 131).

These two questions suggest socialization content focused on metaskills such as adaptability, tolerance for ambiguity and uncertainty, self-awareness, and identity change (Hall, 1987). Individuals have to develop and use these skills rather than depend on the socialization content provided by organizations. Again, mentoring provides the support and encouragement for a mid-career administrator to use and develop these skills.

Routes

Norma's routes on this part of her administrative journey were both similar to and different from the routes at earlier legs of the journey. Her socialization methods are individual, informal, disjunctive, and random and emphasize investiture (Van Maanen & Schein, 1979). Similar to new administrators, mid-career administrators like Norma progress through their socialization alone rather than in groups. The socialization process is seldom formalized by the district and the steps are definitely random. Most mid-career administrators encounter a socialization process for which few role models exist. In Norma's case, her friend provided some support, but no role model on site had traveled the same terrain as she. The school and the district expected Norma to acquire skills, knowledge, and especially values and norms without a role model to guide the process. Because she had previously been a principal, investiture rather than divestiture was more likely to be used in the socialization process. Some divestiture was present, if teachers and administrators perceived Norma as having role conceptions dramatically different from her predecessor.

In addition to these general routes of socialization, mid-career administrators encounter more specific and unique socialization mechanisms. Crow (1993) identified four unique mid-career socialization methods in the literature: exploration, leaving an old role, adjusting role as well as self, and sense making.

Exploration is a major feature of mid-career administrators' socialization. In breaking out of the career routines that have developed by mid-career (Hall, 1986), exploration is essential to identify options. These options, depending on the type of transition(s), may involve alternative school placements, different ways to conceptualize the role, or additional roles to play. The types of alternatives explored may depend on local context and prior socialization (Crow, 1987), as well as larger organizational and societal influences.

A second mechanism of mid-career socialization is leaving the old role (Louis, 1980a). Leaving the old role involves more than simply moving to a new location. It involves a change in self-image and self-esteem (Hall, 1986) and frequently entails a move from perceiving oneself as master over the role to perceiving oneself as a novice (Crow, Levine, & Nager, 1990). Although mid-career administrators have already encountered and, it is to be hoped, mastered the major role requirements, the unique expectations of the new environment start this process over. Leaving the old role may confront the mid-career administrator with feeling a loss of authority while retaining responsibility and a loss of status while moving from veteran to novice (Crow, 1993). The loss of authority is most apparent in intrarole adjustment transitions in which the administrator gives up an old conception of the role, such as sole authority.

A third mid-career socialization mechanism involves adjusting the role as well as the self. We have argued that one of the unique features of mid-career change is that these administrators, unlike their novice counterparts, mold the role to fit their own interests, values, and skills. This does not mean they have total control over molding the role (Miller, 1988). Local school culture is a powerful force for stability over change (Schein, 1992) and limits the job molding that the mid-career administrator may achieve. Yet, mid-career administrators are active participants in the socialization process and much of their action takes the form of molding the role to fit themselves. "Socialization not only presents a world, it constructs one" (Wentworth, 1980, p. 134). Mid-career principals may conceptualize a facilitative role, for example, by making use of prior successful skills, such as using paternalistic methods to teach staff how to make decisions (Crow, 1993). Mid-career administrators adjust the role to fit themselves in ways that fit life and family stage, personal needs, aspirations for the future, and perceptions of the past.

Finally, mid-career socialization involves the use of sense making (Louis, 1980a). Mid-career administrators attempt to make sense of the role when they encounter a new setting, a new role conception, or an additional role. This sense making uses four elements: others' interpretations, local interpretative schemes, predispositions and purposes, and past experiences (Louis, 1980a). Adjusting role and self require each of these elements.

The interpretations and interpretative schemes of teachers, students, parents, superiors, and other administrators regarding how the new administrator and the administrator with a new role concep-tion should act influence how role and self are adjusted. The degree to which these interpretations are homogeneous or heterogeneous, certain or uncertain, can also influence the possibilities for how the role should be enacted. Goldring (1992) found that environmental context, specifically the degree of environmental uncertainty, affects change in the way administrators enact the role, for example, as re-source receiver versus resource mobilizer. The mid-career adminis-trator also has predispositions and purposes regarding such ele-ments as the process of change, the nature of authority, the role of the follower, and the relationship to the community (Crow, 1993). Fi-nally, the mid-career administrator's past experiences interact with the new knowledge, skills, dispositions, and relationships in ways that make the new role and role conception unique.

Destinations

"Points of a journey do not matter when the journey has no des-tination, only an end" (Amis, 1984, quoted in Nicholson & West, 1989, p. 196). The goal of mid-career socialization is not simply an end to the administrative journey. Norma's administrative journey during this mid-career section points to significant destinations for her view of self; the role she performs, both in the school and the association; and the organizations she serves.

Two major types of adjustment occur in work role transitions and present two types of goals: personal development and role de-velopment (Nicholson, 1984; Nicholson & West, 1989). Nicholson (1984) argued that these two outcomes are based on alternatives for adapting to the environmental demands or manipulating the envi-ronment to meet personal requirements. "The reasonable man [sic] adapts himself to the world; the unreasonable one persists in trying to adapt the world to himself. Therefore all progress depends on the unreasonable man [sic]" (George Bernard Shaw, quoted in Nichol-son, 1984, pp. 174-175).

Personal development occurs when "change is absorbed through the person altering his or her frame of reference, values, or other identity-related attributes" (Nicholson, 1984, p. 175). Several studies have pointed to the ways individuals who take on new roles change their personal identity. In a classic study of workers' attitudes to-ward union and management, Lieberman (1956) found that workers' attitudes shifted toward more prounion positions when they became shop stewards and toward more promanagement positions when they became foremen. The attitudes, however, reverted back to original values when they left these roles.

As mid-career administrators take on new roles, move to new schools, or change their role conceptions, they also change their self-images (Hall, 1986). This may be one reason for the hesitancy to take on these role identities—fear of losing the self-esteem or self-image to which one is accustomed.

Role development occurs "when the person tries to change role requirements so that they better match his or her needs, abilities, and identity" (Nicholson, 1984, p. 175). Nicholson argued that role development is also a form of organizational development because the individual is attempting to change objectives, methods, materials, scheduling, and the interpersonal relationships essential to the job.

When Norma became principal of Dayton, she encountered teachers who did not respond to her facilitative style. She nevertheless tried to define her role based on these previously developed conceptions. Martha, the veteran teacher, urged her to be more directive and suggested a developmental way in which Norma could eventually return to this preferred role conception. In this view, Norma could temporarily change the way she enacted the role but maintain a role conception that allowed her to return to the more preferred facilitative style.

Nicholson (1984) identified four adjustment modes based on personal and role development: replication, absorption, determination, and exploration. Replication is a "minimal adjustment to personal and role systems" (p. 175). Absorption involves adjustment only by the person with little modification of the role. Determination is altering the role while leaving the person unaffected. Exploration occurs when "there is simultaneous change in personal qualities and role parameters" (p. 176). Hart (1993) argued that any of these outcomes may be either functional or dysfunctional, depending on the organization's needs. We would add: also depending on the mid-career administrator's needs.

The negotiation of personal and role development issues in the mid-career socialization process provides an opportunity for the development of dynamic leaders for learning communities. As administrators, teachers, students, and parents work through the job molding and personal development inherent in mid-career socialization, they have the opportunity to learn new knowledge, skills, behaviors, and values that enhance their individual and collective learning and growth.

A Look Back and a Look Ahead

In this chapter, we have described the socialization context of a leg of the administrative journey that is seldom acknowledged. Yet, it consumes the majority of time on the journey and is critical for achieving dynamic leadership for learning communities.

In the next chapter, we describe mentoring for mid-career principals. This form of mentoring looks very different from the mentoring we have described for other stages of the administrative journey.

9

Creating One's Own Map

Mentoring Mid-Career Administrators

Thus far on the journey, the guide has been a helping hand, providing an accurate map and at times using a strong boot to prod travelers along. Hand, map, and boot concepts of guiding change as the journey progresses. Experienced travelers make their own maps and at times travel without maps. They may still need a helping hand and even some prodding, but the guiding takes a different form at this career stage. In this chapter, we explore the concept of mentoring mid-career administrators, both assistant principals and principals.

The mid-career stage of administration varies for different administrators. Many mid-career administrators have fallen into a survival mode, getting by day by day, no longer seeking power but only trying to hold on to it. Others are less concerned with survival and continue to seek recognition in their work and lives. Some administrators change schools during mid-career and make new adjustments in their roles and within the new school's culture. Other mid-career administrators stay in the same school for years and become part of the culture.

Mid-career administrators have excessive demands and requirements associated with the job that take away from their effectiveness. They take on more projects and programs as they progress in their careers. Other administrators, including those in the district office, expect more leadership from them and often delegate additional assignments. Thus, mid-career administrators seldom have time for thoughtful analysis of their practices or decisions. They operate alone, seldom receiving helpful and appropriate feedback concerning their job performance. Leithwood (1992) observed, "We know, for example, that principals' activities are typically characterized by brevity, fragmentation, and variety. Rarely, it seems, do principals spend more than ten minutes at a time on a single task, and they make about 150 decisions in the course of an average day" (p. 98).

The typical assumption by many educators is that since mid-career administrators have been around schools for a while they need no special mentoring to help them (Daresh & Playko, 1993). Often, the administrator who admits needing help is perceived as ineffective. We contend that mid-career administrators who ask for mentoring show strength instead of weakness. Dynamic administrators are those who seek help and ideas from others, especially in their own development and in the school's progress.

Kram (1985) reported that individuals in mid-career are no longer establishing competence and defining an occupational identity. Instead, they are adjusting self-images now that they are no longer novices. Questions about one's competence in relation to peers and subordinates surface. For those who are satisfied with their accomplishments, it may be a time of shifting creative energies away from advancement concerns to interests about leisure time and family commitments. Alternately, for those who are dissatisfied with their accomplishments, it may be a time of self-doubt and a sense of urgency as they realize that life is half over and their careers have been well determined.

In this chapter, we follow the same model we have used in previous chapters to describe mentoring. We first discuss mile markers, directions, and destinations and then explore the terrain and routes of mentoring.

Mile Markers

Administrators' mid-career occurs after they have mastered the basic knowledge, skills, behaviors, and values of the role and before they prepare for retirement. This period can involve a considerable length of time in an administrator's career, depending on entry and departure. Mentoring should occur any time during the mid-career period. Mentors of mid-career administrators often have longer relationships with their protégés than do mentors at other career stages.

In the previous chapter, we identified the variety of mid-career transitions that occur, including changing schools, adding extra roles, and adjusting role conception. During the mid-career period, any of these transitions can occur and the administrator may relate to different mentors for different transitions. For example, mid-career principals may have peer mentors who help in changing schools and other peer mentors who help in adjusting to more facilitative styles. Thus, the mile markers created by these transitions may create not only longer-term mentoring relationships but a greater variety of relationships than at previous stages.

Different mentors may help at different stages of the mid-career socialization process. For example, a mid-career assistant principal may choose one mentor for help in exploring alternatives for expanding the role conception and another mentor as guide in working through the process of leaving the old role image. Thus, multiple mentors guide the mid-career administrator through different socialization stages necessary in making the transitions.

Directions

During mid-journey, most travelers rely on the guide less as a teacher, coach, and motivator and more as a friend, comrade, and colleague. Most of what the guide is able to teach has been taught. In fact, the travelers often embark on their own, traveling with each other and becoming guides to each other. In the case study, Norma and Sue were peer mentors who guided each other through professional, career, and psychosocial issues.

In Chapter 1, we suggested that administrators rely on primary mentors more in early career stages than later. Because the administrator networks with others, however, the number of secondary mentors increases as the administrator matures in the profession. Peer relationships develop in each of the career stages, and by mid-career, administrators often have numerous peers who are available as mentors.

Our discussion of mentoring sources in mid-career deals with peer mentors. Peer mentor relationships differ in several ways from most other kinds of mentor-protégé relationships at other career stages.

1. *Expert-novice.* Peer mentors are generally considered equals. Peers do not expect one administrator to have more expertise than another administrator, but together they have expertise that can be beneficial for all.

2. *Older-younger.* Age has no significance in matching peer mentors. Although one peer may be older than another, it is not the older mentor-younger protégé norm that is prevalent at other career stages. Generally, peer mentors tend to be more similar than different in age.

3. *Dyadic.* Peer mentoring is not limited to a dyadic relationship of one mentor with one protégé. An administrator may have several peer mentors who may or may not be associated with each other. Peer mentors may work together in group mentoring, a process in which a team of administrators collaborate on certain problems and concerns.

4. *Career level.* Although peer mentoring is possible at all four career stages, it is most prevalent in the mid-career stage. Peer mentoring may be the only type of mentoring that is effective with mid-career administrators in a long-term commitment.

5. *Primary/secondary.* Most peer mentors are not typically primary mentors. They are not as involved in all three functions as mentors in earlier career stages. Usually, peer mentors tend to be secondary mentors for administrators.

6. *Ad hoc.* Some peer mentor relationships emerge for special reasons, such as developing a particular skill or practice. When the participants have met that purpose, the relationship may end until another need emerges. An example of an ad hoc peer mentor relationship is a group of administrators working together on a district pilot program on site-based management. The group assists each other in planning, implementing, and assessing the site-based management models being used.

Peer mentors can emerge from a variety of sources, including fellow mid-career administrators. Some peer mentor relationships, however, have developed between mid-career administrators and district office personnel, university professors, and former administrators. Peer mentor relationships can emerge between administrators and teachers, as in the case study with Norma and Martha. Not all peer relationships, however, are peer mentor relationships. Most peer relationships are informal and do not involve mentoring. These relationships are better labeled as collegial or friendship. Typically, peer mentors guide each other through all three functions—professional, career, and psychosocial development.

The peer mentor relationship is important because it fosters a connection between two or more mid-career administrators. This relationship may form slowly over time, being needed more at particular times than others. Peer mentor relationships require a high level of trust and must be strong enough to survive challenges. Typically, these challenges are interpersonal conflicts that strain the relationship but usually do not destroy it.

Peer mentor relationships often develop informally with administrators seeking relationships and alliances with others. Hearing others' concerns is comforting and telling one's own story is liberating. Beyond informal peer mentoring, we promote a more formalized approach. The district should develop a peer mentor program, sufficiently supported so that all mid-career administrators are encouraged to participate. We discuss this type of program development in the next chapter.

Destinations

The goal of mid-career mentoring is attaining dynamic leadership. At this career stage, some administrators are already dynamic leaders who appreciate continual mentoring whereas others need mentoring to assist them in becoming dynamic leaders. With this latter type of administrator, changing those who have been established at what they have been doing over time is difficult. After all, bad habits are hard to break. Mark Twain, a disciple of cigars who was disdainful of those who made a great deal about giving up smoking, often claimed that it was quite easy to quit: "I've done it a hundred times!" Mid-career administrators often look at innovation in a similar way, claiming they have changed when they have not. The mid-career administrator who is reluctant to make significant change may need to be resocialized to become a dynamic leader who can embrace real change.

Before we cast dark shadows on mid-career administrators who are not dynamic leaders, we should remember that when mid-career administrators began their journey the destination looked a lot different from the way it looks now. Principals must now change from "implementors to initiators, from a focus on process to a concern for outcomes, from risk avoiders and conflict managers to risk takers. . . . They must learn to lead not from the apex of the organizational pyramid but from the nexus of a web of interpersonal relationships" (Beck & Murphy, 1993, p. 191). This new type of leadership is quite different from that for which many mid-career principals were trained and socialized.

The importance of the administrator in the school has repeatedly been affirmed in the literature. For example, Teddlie and Stringfield (1993) concluded that ineffective principals not surprisingly defined their roles and influence as limited, passive, and bureaucratic. Effective principals, however, held multiple goals for schooling, possessed processes and means of achieving these goals, and were involved in ongoing classroom activities.

Furthermore, with the current emphasis on reform and change in education, the need for improving communication and perceptions about education is essential. Reform will not occur in schools that are narrow and confining in vision and purpose. If mid-career principals are to participate and lead in this educational reform effort, they must have the support of peers to develop the knowledge, skills, behaviors, and values of dynamic leadership.

Peer Mentoring for Professional Development

Peer mentoring is a tool to encourage mid-career administrators to be more dynamic and reflective. Frequently, the job constraints inhibit this kind of professional development unless administrators intentionally prod themselves. Mid-career administrators develop more effectively through a network of other mid-career administrators who share similar problems, concerns, and goals; who resolve complex problems; and who use opportunities for mutual feedback and reflection.

Terrain

If innovation is an important element in schools led by dynamic leaders, then the content of peer mentoring should focus on learning that contributes to innovation. Peer mentoring for innovative professional development includes knowledge of the change process; skills needed for transforming schools; behaviors of adaptability, tolerance, and perseverance; and values of a learning community. Furthermore, peer mentors should learn the knowledge and skills involved with collaborative problem solving, public relations, and communication. Assuming that dynamic leadership is the goal, mid-career administrators need others with whom to share, reflect, and collaborate concerning the change process.

Routes

Sharing. Peer mentors share goals with others who have similar goals. Through sharing, they validate their own goals and explore new goals. Peers, such as Norma and Sue in the case study, share joys and frustrations, successes and failures, constraints and opportunities that emerge with innovation and change. As peers communicate with each other, they often find consolation and relief from isolation. They develop a sense of camaraderie knowing that others have similar experiences. Peers support and prod each other in continued goal making and innovations.

Peers also share new and risky ideas for improving schools and receive confirmation of those ideas. They validate the ideas, which influences whether the individual proceeds to implement the idea or tries other ideas.

Other elements of sharing involve leadership activities such as curriculum development, staff development, clinical supervision, and teacher evaluation. Many routine elements that mid-career administrators manage need creative boosts. Mid-career administrators use peers to find new and better ways of doing routine activities.

Sharing professional development activities is also an important method for peer mentors. Attending workshops and conferences and sharing books and journals with peers boosts mid-career administrators' desire to implement the ideas they find. Through sharing graduate studies, peers also encourage other peers to pursue and complete their education.

Reflecting. Peer mentors reflect together on managerial tasks so that they can improve their practice. Often, these tasks consist of traditional routines that neither meet the school's present needs nor allow leaders to innovate. Reflecting is a method of analyzing and questioning these routine tasks. For example, reflecting on such tasks as course scheduling, budgeting, and building maintenance can help produce new and better ways of performing these tasks that achieve more important goals.

Often, reflection creates spinoffs whereby good ideas foster new ideas. As administrators reflect on their own behaviors and hear about peers' experiences, new ideas emerge. Creativity is often taking others' ideas and reflecting on how they can be used in a new setting. Indeed, some of the most creative ideas come from others who can see what the administrator can not see.

Storytelling also involves reflecting. As we discussed in previous chapters, administrators often swap stories about their experiences. Through reflection on these stories with peers, new knowledge and behaviors emerge.

Collaborating. Collaborating can be a new behavior for mid-career administrators who were socialized to be solo decision makers. In most schools today, and probably more so in the future, collaborative decision making is a skill and a behavior expected of all administrators. Inspiring peers to learn collaborative behaviors requires resocialization. A collaborative approach can assist mid-career administrators in solving problems. Peers have had similar concerns and problems and can suggest solutions and methods for helping an administrator. Collaboration through peer mentor teams can also help solve district concerns and problems.

Peer Mentoring for Career Development

Terrain and Routes

Mentoring administrators to advance in the profession is not as applicable in schools as in the private sector, which usually has opportunities to advance in position, salary, and status. In school leadership, relatively few advancement opportunities exist beyond

the principalship. In previous chapters, we suggested that other career considerations exist for administrators. Here, we explore three
areas of career development in mid-career: lateral career movement,
outside career considerations, and career role adjustment. In career
development, peer mentors explore, reflect, counsel, and advise with
other mid-career administrators.

Lateral Career Movement. In the case study introducing Chapter 8,
Norma moved from an elementary school in one district to an elementary school in a neighboring district. She made her transition
because of a challenge: She wanted some way to display her talents
and experiences. Her new elementary school provided that kind of
challenge.

Mid-career administrators can consider various types of lateral
career movements. We suggested several examples of this type of
movement in Chapter 7 for new administrators who need to consider future career development opportunities. Although mid-career
administrators are not necessarily looking at career development opportunities in the same way new administrators are, many of them
need a career change to boost their self-image and esteem. Hall
(1986) suggested that mid-career individuals need prompting to
break up their career routines. Peer mentors can trigger consideration of lateral career changes.

Lateral career changes for mid-career administrators involve
such opportunities as moving to a different school at the same level
(elementary to elementary), moving to a different school level (middle school to elementary), moving to a different school in a different
socioeconomic area, making an urban-suburban-rural change, moving to a school with a larger or smaller population, or moving to a
school with a different or better reputation. Norma wanted a new
career challenge. She felt she had expertise and experience that could
help a more troubled school. Other reasons mid-career administrators may want to consider lateral movements are location, new
experiences, opportunities to meet new people, opportunities for
recognition, and opportunities for career advancement.

Before making the change, Norma discussed the career move
with Sue, a longtime friend and peer mentor. Peer mentors such as
Norma and Sue explore, reflect, counsel, and advise each other to
consider new positions, administrator and family mobility, political
and social climate of both the old and new school, and both schools'

reputations. Peers also explore and reflect on the possibilities of lateral career movements by procuring further information, such as by visiting the new school and community and chatting with parents and patrons. Making a lateral career move is a big decision in an administrator's life, one that can benefit from peer reflection.

Outside Career Considerations. Mid-career transitions for administrators often involve a different focus for the administrator's outside work life. The precept that career always comes first is often challenged by individuals as they approach midlife. In earlier years, when the administrator's family was more mobile, career opportunities were viewed differently. Mid-career administrators consider such factors as immediate family needs (e.g., a spouse's career, older children's schooling), aging parents' needs, home and neighborhood, leisure activities, church involvement, and friends. These considerations can be explored with peer mentors. Too often, without peer exploration, an administrator may not see all of the implications that affect his or her personal life when considering career transitions.

Norma exemplified another outside career interest when she was elected as the president of the state principals' association. Mid-career administrators may engage in outside career interests such as professional, civic, and political activities. Others teach at local colleges and universities. With each position comes various demands, conflicts, and challenges that affect the administrator's career development.

Career Role Adjustment. Mid-career socialization involves adjusting self and career role. At this leg of the journey, administrators often adjust their role to fit self rather than adjust self to fit the role. Although limitations exist, mid-career administrators have latitude to modify the role that administrators at other career levels do not have. For example, a veteran middle school principal may adjust the role to be more involved in grant writing and fund-raising than in student affairs, curriculum, and instruction, which could be delegated to assistant principals. This choice may be more pronounced in mid-career because of experience, seniority, respect, and personal interest. Adjusting the role to fit self can produce both self-enhancement and increased anxiety. Adjusting the role as a solo activity can be troublesome socially and politically. Peer mentoring can provide advice and counsel about the social, political, and career implications.

Peer Mentoring for
Psychosocial Development

Terrain and Routes

As they travel on their journey, mid-career administrators see change and react to it in different ways. Many fear that their travels will require them to let go of their old ways and take on new ones. For some, traveling toward a new destination can be a difficult challenge, completed only after considerable turmoil. The pressures prove too great for some and they turn back to the haven of home. For others, ready to make changes in their lives, the new journey brings a welcome freshness.

Changing a role in mid-career involves two types of conflict. First, changing to a new school involves more than accepting the position. With the move comes role ambiguity that includes several potential factors. The predecessor's role and reputation affect the expectations of the successor. The mid-career administrator's self-image can be affected in the struggle over adjusting self to meet the expectations created by the predecessor. Role ambiguity involves leaving the comfort zone that the administrator has found in an existing role and moving into a potentially threatening role. Even administrators with high self-esteem feel threatened under unfamiliar conditions. Mid-career administrators who take on new roles or move to new schools change their self-esteem (Hall, 1986).

The second type of role conflict involves remaining in the same position but changing a comfortable role as new developments occur. These changes in the administrator's role involve changes in self, because the administrators are leaving perceived expertise to become a novice again. Many mid-career administrators reject innovations because of the discomfort they cause in the administrator's self-image and self-respect. Often, mid-career administrators believe that if they postpone change long enough, the need for innovation will pass. Sadly, with this postponement change becomes such an obstacle that innovators may eventually give up. Of course, many mid-career administrators embrace the innovative role because it brings new life to them and their careers.

Whatever type of role change that occurs, role ambiguity and conflict often follow. At this time, peer mentors are important supporters and counselors. Although peer mentors have not always experienced the same role change, they can be involved in listening and reflecting. Mid-career administrators making role changes find support and camaraderie important for possible self-image changes. Peer mentoring involves reflecting, questioning, and celebrating in order to help those involved in role changes.

Counselors assume that people can learn about themselves through the process of relating to another person. The counselor is careful to respect the client's perceptions and not to impose personal assumptions. Similarly, peer mentors use inquiry and questioning as tools of reflection to help peers understand old roles, explore new roles, and raise their awareness of how they fit with those roles.

Although we have not introduced celebration in connection with other career stages, it nevertheless is a part of most mentor-protégé relationships. Celebrating with peer mentors can be an important socialization method. Often, mid-career administrators are not recognized for their performance or achievements. Isolation among all educators and especially administrators probably contributes to this lack of celebration. Peer mentors provide meaningful socialization in psychosocial development through celebrations. Peer mentoring enhances self-esteem and self-identity by giving other mid-career administrators assurance, validity, and recognition through celebration. Celebrations also promote continued positive behavior in role assignments. If mid-career administrators receive recognition for their behaviors through celebrations, they often repeat those behaviors.

Celebrations involve private and public activities for peer mentors. Private celebrations include lunch or dinner engagements, sending letters or cards, or making unannounced visits to the school. A private celebration is a validating gesture for the peer. Public celebrations include an announcement at a district administrator meeting, an article written for the district newsletter, or a press release to the local media. Gestures of recognition are often overlooked if a peer does not initiate them.

Psychosocial development is the most ignored element in administrator socialization. Psychosocial well-being affects the mid-career administrator's professional and career development, however. It also plays an important role in creating dynamic leadership. Unless peers validate what is right, mid-career administrators may never explore new roles or attempt to make schools better places for kids.

A Look Back and a Look Ahead

Mentoring mid-career administrators is probably the most over-looked aspect of mentoring. In this chapter, we described how peer mentoring can serve the three functions of professional, career, and psychosocial development to encourage the development of dynamic leaders.

In the next chapter, we describe how mentor programs can be established to implement the mentoring ideas from the four career stages. We include issues of planning, selection, training, and evaluation.

10

Shifting Into High Gear

Establishing Mentor Programs

The adventure of traveling, seeing new places, meeting new people, and experiencing new cultures can be an exhilarating experience. This adventure includes not only the guides and travelers we have emphasized thus far but passengers who contribute to the total experience. Earlier, we suggested that passengers included such groups as university faculty and district office administrators, who have an interest in the journey through allocation of resources, development, and assessment. In this chapter, we discuss the role of university and district office personnel in establishing mentor programs.

We propose that mentoring be used for principals' professional development using the information that we have presented in this book. University principal preparation programs and school districts—working collaboratively when appropriate—should develop mentor programs for interns, new assistant principals, new principals, and mid-career principals

Mentor programs for school principals are not common. Cohn and Sweeney (1992) contacted 40 school districts in Southern California and found only 8 that had any kind of mentor programs for principals. The eight programs were primarily informal in structure and had often been established by one individual who had a particular interest and belief in mentoring.

Although typically principals either seek their own mentors or mentors emerge, we believe that leaving mentoring to chance is undesirable. Informal mentor relationships are important but do not serve the growing need for dynamic leadership in today's schools. Indeed, principals who seek mentors are doing the right thing and should continue to do so, but all principals need mentors, not just those who are in the right places at the right times. Our argument therefore is for school district administrators to develop formal mentor programs for new assistant principals and new principals and peer mentor programs for mid-career principals. We also urge university departments preparing school leaders to develop formal internships that include mentor programs. In developing mentor and internship programs, we suggest five components: (a) organizational planning, (b) mentor selection, (c) mentor training, (d) mentor and protégé matching, and (e) evaluation.

Organizational Planning

Planning the mentor program is essential before implementation begins. A solid foundation must exist and all parties included in the mentor program should be included in the planning. We suggest that districts and university personnel consider the journey metaphor developed in this book. We used the metaphor to help the reader understand component parts of school principals' socialization, especially through the means of mentoring. The journey metaphor can also be used with program planning in considering mile markers (time), directions (sources), terrain (content), routes (methods), and destinations (goals).

Program planners need to consider certain practical and managerial aspects in developing the mentor program. We suggest those involved in planning consider the following questions:

- Who will serve on the program planning team?
- Who will direct/coordinate/supervise the mentor (or internship) program?
- What will be the expense of the program?
- How will the program be announced to those involved?
- How will mentors be selected?

- How will mentors be trained? Who will facilitate the initial training? Who will facilitate continued mentor training and support sessions?
- How will mentors and protégés be "matched"? How will they be "unmatched" if a pairing does not work?
- How will mentors and protégés be introduced to each other?
- How will the mentor relationship be monitored?
- How will the mentor program be evaluated? Who will be the evaluator? How will the evaluation data be disseminated?
- How will celebrations and rewards be given?

Mentor Selection

The selection of principals as mentors is a key element for the program's success. Several factors need to be considered in selecting mentors. First, mentors should exemplify good school leadership. They need to be highly regarded educators and leaders with strong character reputations and well respected in the community. Indeed, if the goal of mentoring is developing dynamic leaders, then the mentor-principal must be recognized as a dynamic leader. Second, principals should be selected who are committed to the concept of mentoring and to the training necessary to be a better mentor. Some excellent principals are not willing or available to commit themselves to receiving training or fulfilling mentoring expectations in an effective manner. These principals do not make good mentors. Third, principal mentors should be selected who are learners themselves and engage others in learning. We have distinguished dynamic leaders who cultivate learning communities as the goal of mentoring. A mentor who does not model learning is not an effective guide for this destination. Last, principals should be selected who have the time for mentoring. Although committed to mentoring, even the best principals can become involved in so many programs that they lack the time for effectively mentoring others.

Mentor Training

In our journey metaphor, we emphasize the active role to be taken by the guide to ensure a safe and memorable experience. A guide is not someone who is only around on demand and rescues the travelers when called upon. Mentoring, similarly, is not a passive activity and requires the mentor to be actively engaged with the protégé. Accomplishing the goal of dynamic leadership, however, does not come easily. The skills needed to carry out this mentoring process must be learned and practiced.

Research has suggested mentor training does help in the mentoring process. In two separate studies, mentors who had been trained in mentoring had a higher level of mentoring activity and protégés rated their relationship with trained mentors significantly higher (Cohn & Sweeney, 1992). Walker and Stott (1993) proposed that the ability to carry out the mentor role productively does not usually come naturally and that mentors need some form of training. Walker and Stott suggested that mentor training is more important than selecting mentors with certain qualifications.

Based on our experience in training mentors, we suggest program facilitators consider three stages of mentor training: selection and training of trainers, annual orientation, and mentor workshops.

Selection and Training of Trainers

We have consistently found that the best mentor trainers are mentor-principals. They bring to the training workshops experience, firsthand knowledge, and stories that captivate other principals. Mentor-principals as trainers use learning activities that other mentors view as realistic. Mentors also see the trainers' enthusiasm and commitment to the mentoring process. Although university and district personnel should be involved with goals and curriculum, mentor-principals should do most of the training. Mentors are more attentive in listening and learning from their peers than from district or university personnel. Furthermore, as mentors learn to be trainers, they become more enthusiastic and committed to the mentoring process.

Mentor training involves understanding adult learning. Trainers must acknowledge mentors' learning styles. It is important that trainers appreciate this diversity of thinking and learning styles. Adult learners create their own meaning and apply the mentor training in ways that are effective for them. Adult learners dislike recipes that oversimplify mentoring processes.

Trainers should teach key elements of mentoring and then allow each mentor to reflect and internalize the elements within his or her own context. We have found workshop sessions are better received when trainers do four things: (a) outline a mentoring concept (content and methods) and relate it to actual practice (e.g., storytelling), (b) engage mentors to share their own experiences with the concept in small groups or with the entire group, (c) engage mentors in practicing the concept in simulations or other feedback activities, and (d) help mentors internalize the concept by writing and reflecting about it.

Annual Mentor Training Orientations

Orientations are annual events that have two purposes. First, the orientation allows *new* mentors to gain an understanding of the mentoring process and the district and university philosophy, goals, and expectations. Second, the annual orientation allows *all* mentors to review the mentoring process and reflect on changes that may be needed for the year. We propose that the orientation allow mentors to learn and discuss the mentoring elements presented in Chapter 1, such as the meaning of mentoring, the definition of mentoring, the goals and definition of dynamic leadership, and mentoring pitfalls and benefits.

The orientation also includes a basic understanding of protégés' socialization. A knowledge of how protégés learn the role, adjust to the school environment, and internalize the school's values helps make the mentor's work fit the needs of the protégé and the school.

Orientations also serve as a time for mentors to learn about protégés, in particular, the protégé with whom a mentor will be associated. Learning about the protégés helps mentors begin planning for time, locations, content, and methods.

Mentor Training Workshops

Mentor workshops follow annual orientations to provide regular and consistent support, training, and quality control. The number of workshops and timing vary with the type of mentoring, that is, interns, new assistant principals and principals, or mid-career administrators. In initiating mentor training workshops, three elements are considered: what to mentor (content), how to mentor (methods), and assessment of mentoring. Content involves the knowledge, skills, behaviors, and values of learning dynamic school leadership. Content includes teaching both technical and cultural aspects. The technical aspects are "how things are done," whereas the cultural aspects are "how things are done around here," for example, how things are done in the context of the values and standards of this community.

Training mentors in the methods they use with protégés involves teaching and explaining as well as practice through simulations such as role playing and case studies. Simulations are effective learning activities for mentors to practice and reflect on their mentoring methods. For example, we use role-playing to train mentors in giving feedback to protégés. Using a triad approach, individuals take the roles of mentor, protégé, and observer. Short scenarios are given in which the individual in the mentor role practices the concept of giving feedback to a protégé. The protégé responds to the feedback and the observer takes notes on the process. After the simulation, the observer reports what was said and done. The triad then reflects on the process and determines what was done well by the mentor and what could have been done differently. The individuals switch roles and a new scenario begins. In this way, mentors not only learn about a mentoring method but practice the method and assess it.

Matching Mentors and Protégés

Guides and travelers come to the journey in two ways, either by chance as they travel together on the same road or by mutual choice—through planning the journey together. Likewise, significant mentor relationships form because of happenstance or through the mutual planned choice of the mentor and the protégé, particularly where they have a high regard for one another. Mentor relationships form best when mentors and protégés share a similar style of thinking (Parkay, 1988). Roche (1979) found that many mentor relationships in the business world develop into lengthy friendships. Almost half of all respondents in this study reported that if they had a mentor they continued to have a relationship with that person.

The most effective mentor relationships are those in which the partners are allowed to choose each other freely (Zey, 1985). "People tend to increase their interactions with those similar to themselves and limit their actions with those with whom they feel dissimilar" (Hart, 1993, p. 35). Choice of mentors by protégés may not be possible, practical, or even desirable in all settings. The best results are achieved when balance between choice and developmental needs is facilitated.

Consideration should be given to matching mentors' and protégés' styles and ideologies. A new principal or administrative intern who is enthusiastic about school leadership and has an informal, open, and creative style will be better mentored by a like-minded mentor than by someone whose style is more conservative.

Evaluation

Several types of evaluation should be used as part of any mentor program. First, a comprehensive program evaluation should be conducted for all parties involved in the program. The participating mentors and protégés should give careful consideration to evaluating mentoring content and methods. We recommend both a confidential instrument administered to the mentors and protégés and selective interviews with those willing to give frank and open feedback.

A second type of evaluation is a needs assessment for program modifications. As the profession of educational leadership transforms, as student demographics change, and as other district and school needs and visions change, continual efforts for renewal need to be made in the mentor program.

A third type of evaluation obtains feedback on the quantity and quality of mentoring in the program. Hay (1995) identified several problems with gaining this information: (a) it can be intrusive and time-consuming to observe mentoring sessions, (b) protégés may be reluctant to evaluate their mentors if the mentors influence the protégés' future career prospects, and (c) uncooperative or incompetent protégés may unfairly evaluate their mentors.

Sponsoring organizations such as districts and universities should evaluate the quality and quantity of mentoring. Protégés should be asked to respond to the quality and quantity of mentoring and to make recommendations to help mentors be more effective with future protégés.

Mentor evaluation of protégés should be excluded from the mentoring process (Cohn & Sweeney, 1992). If this suggestion is followed, a supervisor of a protégé should not serve as a mentor. The mentor-protégé relationship should be built on a climate of trust, which could be adversely affected if evaluation is part of the process. Furthermore, since mentoring is a method of socialization, any evaluation by mentors should be limited to those areas in which the mentor can help the protégé develop. This limited evaluation should not be shared with anyone except in rare situations when the safety and well-being of children are in question.

Mentor Program Considerations for Each Career Stage

The elements of developing effective mentor programs previously described are generic to mentoring protégés at all career stages. Socialization, and therefore mentoring, has unique features depending on the part of the administrative journey being traveled.

Principal Interns

Internships have been one of the weaker aspects of university preparation programs. Many universities do not require an internship experience of their students, and if required these internships are often poorly supervised and monitored:

> Too often field sites are chosen haphazardly and/or are not closely monitored. The potential for interns being constrained to passive observation, being placed in roles that do not fit closely with their career goals, or being used as "go-fers," is great when clear and agreed upon expectations are not developed. Likewise, campus based practicums and seminars on a regular basis are rarely available or required and clinical experiences are often isolated from the rest of a student's program flow. Finally, the connecting linkages between on campus experiences and field based experiences are rarely adequately developed. (Milstein, 1990, p. 121)

University preparation programs should not bear the entire weight of the blame for neglect in internship requirements. Most states do not require an internship for administrative certification, and therefore university programs and school districts are not inclined to implement internships. Furthermore, school districts have seldom used internships as a basis for recruitment or hiring.

The most common internship programs are offered by universities (Milstein, Bobroff, & Restine, 1991). Some school districts have developed their own internship programs for aspiring principals. We believe the best approach is for university preparation programs and school districts to form cooperative arrangements.

As we suggested in Chapter 4, we believe that the best internships for aspiring principals are those that are yearlong, full-time experiences in which the interns are paid the equivalent of their teaching salary. Under such arrangements, school districts and universities select and place interns with qualified mentors in schools that need additional assistant principals. Instead of hiring a new assistant principal for the year, the school district places an intern in the open position. The salary line goes to the intern and allows the district and university to socialize and assess the intern for future administrative openings.

Partial internships can also be valuable for those individuals who cannot pursue a full-time experience. Partial internships involve either part-day or part-year experiences. For example, an individual may be in a school as an intern for half a day and teach the other half. Again, the key to effective partial internships is the quality of the mentoring.

Selecting sites for internships should depend mostly on the mentor's qualifications at the site and the intern's interests. Requiring interns to have both elementary and secondary school internships adds to the global educational outlook of the intern and gives the intern a variety of mentor perspectives on leadership. We also discourage individuals from fulfilling their internships at the school where they teach. Returning to the same school limits the intern's experience to one leadership style and philosophy.

Mentors must keep in mind unique considerations in working with interns. The mentor must realize that the intern's university responsibilities at times conflict with administrative duties. For example, the intern probably cannot attend to some duties because of class schedules or the need for study time. Mentors also should be aware of course work so they can make theory-to-practice connections. Some universities appoint intern mentors as adjunct professors and include them in program planning. Finally, mentors need to give the time necessary for mentoring the intern. Effective mentoring needs both quality and quantity of time. In fact, district administrators should assign mentors fewer district responsibilities and projects.

New Assistant Principal and Principals

Beginning assistant principals and principals need regular and specific feedback on their performance. The main consideration for mentor programs for new assistant principals and principals is training mentors to have regular reflective conferences with the newcomers. Knowing how to give feedback is a critical mentoring method for those working with newcomers to the district.

Program facilitators should consider three other issues in developing mentor programs for new assistant principals and principals. They should consider arranging schedules of both the newcomer and the mentor so that time is available for these conferences. Because new administrators have not yet developed efficient routines, those involved in the mentor program must be flexible and sensitive to new administrators' schedules.

Unlike interns, new assistant principals and principals are under contract, which intensifies the risk of mistakes and poor judgment. These administrators are also more open to public scrutiny. Program facilitators therefore need to emphasize to mentors the pressures that new administrators feel and the need for mentors to respond with support, understanding, and suggestions.

One of the strongest feelings that emerges for new administrators is isolation. Few if any other administrators are in the building. New administrators have recently left their teaching reference group and may not yet feel part of the administrative group. Mentor programs need to provide opportunities—both time and location—that promote acceptance by the administrative reference group.

Mid-Career Administrators

Although most mid-career administrators find peer mentors informally, such arrangements are often selective and exclusionary. District administrators can facilitate formal peer mentor arrangements so that all administrators in the district are included. Districts can encourage formal and informal peer mentor groups by arranging times, locations, and resources. Some districts that have employed peer mentor programs have extended district principal meetings so that peer mentors can meet at a regular time and place with peers. Other districts have arranged for principals to visit each other's school to observe peers in action, see new ideas, and reflect on similar problems. These arrangements may require paying travel expenses and hiring substitutes. Often, peers leave their buildings to meet for lunch, refreshments, or walks. These arrangements afford a more relaxed atmosphere with fewer interruptions for the peer mentor process.

Storm Clouds on the Horizon: Meeting the Problems of Mentoring

On the journey, guides, travelers, and passengers have to expect problems along the way. Storm clouds on the horizon have the potential of wreaking havoc on the journey. Clouds can also shade the sun and cool the temperature so traveling is more comfortable. They might even force us to take a needed rest. Such storm clouds occur in establishing mentor programs. They consist of issues, problems, and concerns that if left unnoticed or unaddressed can wreak havoc in the mentoring process. These problems can also prompt needed reflection and further planning to actually enhance the mentor program. We have outlined the following four issues that should be considered in program development.

First, good principals may not be good mentors. The roles of an effective principal and an effective mentor are somewhat different. We believe, however, that good mentors are good principals.

The following situations illustrate how good principals do not always make good mentors:

1. Some principals do not and perhaps cannot give the time it takes for being a mentor. They are busy people involved in many projects and tasks. Their energy is exceeded by no one. They hit the road running in the morning and they continue running much of the day. Having someone to mentor acts as a burden on their day's agenda.

2. Good principals are not always committed to the concept of mentoring. Many do not have enough training to understand mentoring. Others are unable to effectively communicate their philosophy, ideas, and methods of school leadership.

3. Mentoring involves a type of personality that requires patience, understanding, and tolerance. Not all principals have these personality traits. This does not reflect on their ability to be good administrators. In fact, some of the most highly respected principals are not used as mentors simply because of their personality traits.

A second issue for those who establish and coordinate mentor programs is that mentoring expectations may be unrealistically high. The mentoring process is not a rescue effort for poorly performing principals or assistant principals. Although it may help a struggling principal, mentoring should not be considered as the sole method in rehabilitating or reforming marginal principals.

A third storm cloud may emerge that prevents some potentially promising people from having mentors. This phenomenon is what Carruthers (1993) described as the St. Matthew effect. This phrase refers to the situation in which gifted or popular individuals more easily obtain mentors than less gifted, disadvantaged, or minority individuals. The St. Matthew effect comes from Matthew 25:29: "For to everyone that hath shall be given, and he shall abound; but, from him that hath not, that also which he seemeth to have shall be taken away." Biblical scholars will be quick to argue that the scripture has been taken out of context. Nevertheless, the situation, although misnamed, is noteworthy as a mentoring issue to be acknowledged and remedied.

The St. Matthew effect can emerge in several ways. Some principals tend to mentor only those whom they personally like. District administrators often include individuals in mentor programs whom they perceive to be "principal material" or to have the "right look" for a principal. We observed an older, female prospective principal intern whom district administrators initially denied access to the mentoring process. She, however, persisted and found a mentor on her own. District administrators changed their perceptions of her and soon selected her for an assistant principal position.

A fourth issue emerges that is also potentially damaging. Carruthers (1993) named this issue the Salieri phenomenon, based on the story of Salieri, the court composer who acted as musical gatekeeper to keep Mozart from being publicly recognized. When a mentor impedes outstanding individuals from receiving acclaim, the Salieri phenomenon is operating. Principals who operate in this fashion act as gatekeepers in closing opportunities for aspiring, dynamic, and motivated individuals who may be perceived as threatening or upstaging the principal. The consequences of such actions are obvious. The best individuals may never be recognized or promoted. For example, a mentor-principal would not endorse an assistant principal to be in the district's principal candidate pool. The mentor-principal and the assistant disagreed in a disciplinary situation involving a junior high student. The assistant sided with the student and his parents and the principal felt the assistant principal had "caved in." Although the assistant principal had a reputation as a fine teacher before entering administration and a positive experience in another school as an assistant principal, the mentor-principal felt the assistant had not dealt with the discipline action appropriately and prevented his name from being placed in the candidacy pool.

The above problems may never arise, but just as for storm clouds on the horizon, recognizing and forecasting these problems can be critical for the successful development of a mentor program.

Looking Back and Moving Ahead

In this final chapter, we have proposed how formal mentor programs can be developed for the four stages of principal careers. Mentor programs not only socialize principals to become dynamic leaders but also help create better schools that enrich teaching and learning for children.

Moving ahead involves you, the reader. If you are a district office administrator, begin the process of developing a mentor program. If you are a principal or assistant principal, do not wait for your district to develop a mentor program but find a mentor and talk to those who can influence the district to begin a program. If you are a university professor, begin a discussion with other professors on mentoring and internships in your preparation programs. If you are an aspiring principal wanting to enter a principal preparation program, find a university with a strong academic program that includes a concentrated internship component. If you are a researcher, consider further study on the socialization of principals through mentoring.

References

Adkins, C. L. (1990). A longitudinal examination of the organizational socialization process (Doctoral dissertation, University of South Carolina, 1990). *Dissertation Abstracts International, 51,* 2446-A.

Akerlund, P. M. (1988). The socialization of first-year principals and vice-principals (Doctoral dissertation, Seattle University, 1988). *Dissertation Abstracts International, 49,* 2029-A.

Altounyan, C. (1995). *Putting mentors in their place: The role of workplace support in professional education.* Msc HRM dissertation, Sheffield Business School, Sheffield, UK.

Amis, M. (1984). *Money: A suicide note.* London: Jonathan Cape.

Ashby, D., & Maki, D. M. (1996, February). *What first year principals don't know: How you may be able to help new colleagues succeed.* Paper presented at the National Association of Secondary School Principals Annual Convention, San Francisco.

Austin, B. D., & Brown, H. L. (1970). *Report of the assistant principalship: Vol. 3. The study of the secondary school principalship.* Washington, DC: National Association of Secondary School Principals.

Backer, A. B. (1990). *Subordinate socialization into the superior/subordinate dyad: Perceptions of solidarity as a function of perceptions of uncertainty and homophily.* Unpublished master's thesis, San Diego State University, San Diego, CA.

Baker, R. Z. (1990). A control perspective of organizational socialization: Tactics, tolerance for organizational influence, and outcomes for new entrants (Doctoral dissertation, University of California at Los Angeles, 1990). *Dissertation Abstracts International, 51,* 552-A.

Baltzell, D., & Dentler, R. (1983). *Selecting American school principals: Research report.* Cambridge, MA: Abt.

Barnard, C. I. (1938). *The functions of the executive.* Cambridge, MA: Harvard University Press.

Barth, R. S. (1990). *Improving schools from within: Teachers, parents, and principals can make the difference.* San Francisco: Jossey-Bass.

Barth, R. S. (1997). The leader as learner. *Education Week, 26*(23), 42, 56.

Beck, L. G., & Murphy, J. (1993). *Understanding the principalship: Metaphorical themes, 1920's-1990's.* New York: Teachers College Press.

Becker, H. S. (1964). Personal change in adult life. *Sociometry, 27,* 40-53.

Becker, H. S., Geer, B., Hughes, E. C., & Strauss, A. L. (1961). *Boys in white.* Chicago: University of Chicago Press.

Bolman, L. G., & Deal, T. E. (1991). *Reframing organizations.* San Francisco: Jossey-Bass.

Bolton, E. (1980). A conceptual analysis of the mentor relationship in the career development of women. *Adult Education, 30*(4), 195-297.

Brim, O. G. (1966). Socialization through the life cycle. In O. G. Brim & S. Wheeler (Eds.), *Socialization after childhood* (pp. 1-50). New York: John Wiley.

Brown, M. H. (1985). That reminds me of a story: Speech action in organizational socialization. *Western Journal of Speech Communication, 49,* 27-42.

Bullis, C. (1993). Organizational socialization research: Enabling, constraining, and shifting perspectives. *Communication Monographs, 60,* 10-17.

Bullis, C., & Stout, K. (1996, November). *Organizational socialization: A feminist standpoint approach.* Paper presented at annual conference of Speech Communication Association, San Diego, CA.

Cabrera, R., & Sours, M. (1989). Helpful hints for first-year principals. *Principal, 68,* 22-24.

Carlson, R. O. (1972). *School superintendents: Careers and performance.* Columbus, OH: Charles E. Merrill.

Carruthers, J. (1993). The principles and practice of mentoring. In B. J. Caldwell & E. M. A. Carter (Eds.), *The return of the mentor: Strategies for workplace learning* (pp. 9-24). London: Falmer.

Clawson, J. G. (1980). Mentoring in managerial careers. In C. B. Derr (Ed.), *Work, family, and the career* (pp. 144-165). New York: Praeger.

Cogswell, B. E. (1968). Some structural properties influencing socialization. *Administrative Science Quarterly, 13,* 417-440.

Cohn, K. C., & Sweeney, R. C. (1992, April). *Principal mentoring programs: Are school districts providing the leadership?* Paper presented at the annual meeting of the American Educational Research Association, San Francisco. (ERIC Document Reproduction Service No. ED 345 376)

Cordeiro, P. A., & Smith-Sloan, E. (1995, April). *Apprenticeships for administrative interns: Learning to talk like a principal.* Paper presented at the annual meeting of the American Educational Research Association, San Francisco.

Covey, S. R. (1990). *The 7 habits of highly effective people: Powerful lessons in personal change.* New York: Simon & Schuster.

Crow, G. M. (1987). Career mobility of elementary school principals and conflict with the central office. *Urban Review, 19*(3), 139-150.

Crow, G. M. (1990). Central office influence on the principal's relationship with teachers. *Administrator's Notebook, 34*(1), 1-4.

Crow, G. M. (1992). The principal in schools of choice: Middle manager, entrepreneur, and symbol manager. *Urban Review, 24*(3), 165-174.

Crow, G. M. (1993). Reconceptualizing the school administrator's role: Socialization at mid-career. *School Effectiveness and School Improvement, 4*(2), 131-152.

Crow, G. M., & Glascock, C. (1995). Socialization to a new conception of the principalship. *Journal of Educational Administration, 33*(1), 22-43.

Crow, G. M., Levine, L., & Nager, N. (1990). No more business as usual: Career changers who become teachers. *American Journal of Education, 98*(3), 197-223.

Crow, G. M., Matthews, L. J., & McCleary, L. (1996). *Leadership: A relevant and realistic role for principals.* Princeton Junction, NJ: Eye on Education.

Crow, G. M., & Peterson, K. D. (1994). School principals: Role in restructured schools. In T. Husen & T. N. Postlethwaite (Eds.), *International encyclopedia of education* (2nd ed., vol. 9, pp. 5268-5273). Oxford, UK: Pergamon.

Crow, G. M., & Pounders, M. L. (1994, October). *The symbolic nature of the administrative internship: Building a sense of occupational community.* Paper presented at the annual meeting of the University Council for Educational Administration, Philadelphia.

Crow, G. M., & Pounders, M. L. (1995, April). *Organizational socialization of new urban principals: Variations of race and gender.* Paper presented at the annual meeting of the American Educational Research Association, San Francisco.

Crow, G. M., & Pounders, M. L. (1996, April). *The administrative internship: "Learning the ropes" of an occupational culture.* Paper presented at the annual meeting of the American Educational Research Association, New York.

Daloz, L. A. (1983). Mentors: Teachers who make a difference. *Change, 5*(6), 24-27.

Daresh, J. C. (1986). In service for beginning principals: The first hurdles are the highest. *Theory into Practice, 25,* 3.

Daresh, J. C., & Playko, M. A. (1990, April). *Preservice administrative mentoring: Reflections of the mentors.* Paper presented at the Annual Meeting of the American Educational Research Association, Boston, MA.

Daresh, J. C., & Playko, M. A. (1992). *The professional development of school administrators: Preservice, induction, and in service applications.* Needham Heights, MA: Allyn & Bacon.

Daresh, J. C., & Playko, M. A. (1993). *Leaders helping leaders: A practical guide to administrative mentoring.* New York: Scholastic.

DuBose, E. (1986). *A study of the task-specific assistance and information needs of incoming elementary school principals in South Carolina.* Unpublished EdD dissertation, University of South Carolina. Columbia.

Duke, D. L. (1987). *School leadership and instructional improvement.* New York: Random House.

Duke, D. L., Isaacson, N. S., Sagor, R., & Schmuck, P. A. (1984). *Transition to leadership: An investigation of the first year of the principalship.* Transition to Leadership Project, Lewis and Clark College, Portland, OR.

Falcione, R. L., & Wilson, C. E. (1988). Socialization processes in organizations. In G. M. Goldhaber & G. A. Barnett (Eds.), *Handbook of organizational communication* (pp. 151-169). Norwood, NJ: Ablex.

Feldman, D. C. (1976). A contingency theory of socialization. *Administrative Science Quarterly, 21,* 433-452.

Feldman, D. C. (1981). The multiple socialization of organization members. *Academy of Management Review, 6,* 309-318.

Ferriero, D. (1982). ARL directors as protégés and mentors. *Journal of Academic Librarianship, 7*(6), 358-365.

Fisher, C. (1986). Organizational socialization: An integrative review. *Research in Personnel and Human Resources Management, 4,* 101-145.

Gecas, V. (1981). Contexts of socialization. In M. Rosenberg & R. Turner (Eds.), *Social psychology: Sociological perspectives* (pp. 165-199). New York: Basic Books.

Gehrke, N. J. (1988). Toward a definition of mentoring. *Theory into Practice, 27*(3), 190-194.

Gehrke, N. J., & Kay, R. S. (1984). The socialization of beginning teachers through mentor-protégé relationships. *Journal of Teacher Education, 35*(3), 21-24.

Geuss, R. R. (1993). The organizational socialization process of first and second career teachers: A study of selected outcomes (Doctoral dissertation, University of Maryland, 1993). *Dissertation Abstracts International, 55,* 935-A.

Glickman, C. D., Gordon, S. P., & Ross-Gordon, J. M. (1995). *Supervision of instruction: A developmental approach* (3rd ed.). Needham Heights, MA: Allyn & Bacon.

Goldring, E. B. (1992). System-wide diversity in Israel: Principals as transformational and environmental leaders. *Journal of Educational Administration, 30*(3), 49-62.

Goldring, E. B., & Rallis, S. F. (1993). *Principals of dynamic schools.* Thousand Oaks, CA: Corwin.

Gouldner, A. W. (1957). Cosmopolitans and locals: I. *Administrative Science Quarterly, 2,* 281-306.

Greenfield, W. D. (1977a). Administrative candidacy: A process of new role learning: Part 1. *Journal of Educational Administration, 15*(1), 30-48.

Greenfield, W. D. (1977b). Administrative candidacy: A process of new role learning: Part 2. *Journal of Educational Administration, 15*(2), 170-193.

Greenfield, W. D. (1985a, April). *Being and becoming a principal: Responses to work contexts and socialization processes.* Paper presented at the annual meeting of the American Educational Research Association, Chicago. (ERIC Documentation Reproduction Service No. ED 254 932)

Greenfield, W. D. (1985b). Developing an instructional role for the assistant principal. *Education and Urban Society, 18*(1), 85-92.

Greenfield, W. D. (1985c). The moral socialization of school administrators: Informal role learning outcomes. *Educational Administration Quarterly, 21*(4), 99-119.

Greenfield, W. D. (1985d). Studies of the assistant principalship: Toward new avenues of inquiry. *Education and Urban Society, 18*(1), 7-27.

Greenfield, W. D., Marshall, C., & Reed, D. B. (1986). Experience in the vice principalship: Preparation for leading schools? *Journal of Educational Administration, 24*(1), 107-121.

Griffiths, D. E., Stout, R. T., & Forsyth, P. B. (Eds.). (1988). *Leaders for America's schools.* Berkeley, CA: McCutchan.

Gross, N. C., & Trask, A. E. (1976). *The sex factor and the management of schools.* New York: John Wiley.

Hall, D. T. (1980). Socialization processes in later career years: Can there be growth at terminal level? In C. B. Derr (Ed.), *Work, family, and the career* (pp. 219-236). New York: Praeger.

Hall, D. T. (1986). Breaking career routines: Mid-career choice and identity development. In D. T. Hall (Ed.), *Career development in organizations* (pp. 120-159). San Francisco: Jossey-Bass.

Hall, D. T. (1987). Careers and socialization. *Journal of Management,* *13*(2), 302-321.

Hart, A. W. (1991). Leader succession and socialization: A synthesis. *Review of Educational Research, 61*(4), 451-474.

Hart, A. W. (1993). *Principal succession: Establishing leadership in schools.* Albany: State University of New York Press.

Hart, A. W., & Bredeson, P. V. (1996). *The principalship: A theory of professional learning and practice.* New York: McGraw-Hill.

Hay, J. (1995). *Transformational mentoring: Creating developmental alliances for changing organizational cultures.* London: McGraw-Hill.

Hess, F. (1985). The socialization of the assistant principal: From the perspective of the local school district. *Education and Urban Society, 18*(1), 93-106.

Holcomb, E. (1989). Beginning elementary principals' perceptions of support provided during their first year of practice. *ERS Spectrum, 7,* 10-16.

Hughes, E. C. (1959). The study of occupations. In R. K. Merton, L. Broom, & L. Cottrell (Eds.), *Sociology today* (pp. 442-458). New York: Basic Books.

Inkeles, A. (1969). Social structure and socialization. In A. Bandura (Ed.), *Principles of behavior modification* (pp. 615-632). New York: Holt, Rinehart & Winston.

Jones, E. H. (1983). *Black school administrators: A review of their early history, trends in recruitment, problems, and needs.* Arlington, VA: American Association of School Administrators.

Jones, G. R. (1983a). Organizational socialization as information processing activity: A life history analysis. *Human Organization, 42*(4), 314-320.

Jones, G. R. (1983b). Psychological orientation and the process of organizational socialization: An interactionist perspective. *Academy of Management Review, 8*(3), 464-474.

Jones, G. R. (1986). Socialization tactics, self-efficacy, and newcomers' adjustments to organizations. *Academy of Management Journal, 29*(2), 262-279.

Kanter, R. (1977). *Men and women of the corporation.* New York: Basic Books.

Katz, R. (1980). Time and work: Toward an integrative perspective. In B. M. Staw & L. L. Cummings (Eds.), *Research in organizational behavior* (Vol. 2, pp. 81-127). Greenwich, CT: JAI.

Kay, R. S. (1990). A definition of developing self-reliance. In T. M. Bey & C. T. Holmes (Eds.), *Mentoring: Developing successful new teachers* (pp. 25-37). Reston, VA: Association of Teacher Educators.

Kram, K. E. (1985). *Mentoring at work: Developmental relationships in organizational life.* Glenview, IL: Scott, Foresman.

Langer, E. J. (1989). *Mindfulness.* Reading, MA: Addison-Wesley.

Leithwood, K. A. (1992). The principal's role in teacher development. In M. Fullan & A. Hargreaves (Eds.), *Teacher development and educational change* (pp. 86-103). London: Falmer.

Levinson, D. J., Darrow, C. N., Klein, E. B., Levinson, M. H., & McKee, B. (1978). *The seasons of a man's life.* New York: Ballantine.

Lieberman, A., & Miller, L. (Eds.). (1991). *Staff development for education in the '90s: New demands, new realities, new perspectives.* New York: Teachers College Press.

Lieberman, S. (1956). The effect of changes in roles on the attitudes of role occupants. *Human Relations, 9,* 385-402.

Lomotey, K. (1989). *African-American principals: School leadership and success.* New York: Greenwood.

London, L. (1985). *Developing managers.* San Francisco: Jossey-Bass.

Long, D. H. (1988). *A study of the socialization process of beginning public school administrators.* Unpublished doctoral dissertation, Vanderbilt University, Nashville, TN.

Lortie, D. C. (1975). *Schoolteacher: A sociological study.* Chicago: University of Chicago Press.

Lortie, D. C., Crow, G. M., & Prolman, S. (1983). *The elementary school principal in suburbia: An occupational and organizational study* (Final Report). National Institute of Education, Washington, DC.

Louis, M. R. (1978). *How MBA graduates cope with early job experiences: An expectation/attribution approach.* Unpublished dissertation, Graduate School of Management, University of California—Los Angeles.

Louis, M. R. (1980a). Surprise and sensemaking: What newcomers experience in entering unfamiliar organizational settings. *Administrative Science Quarterly, 25,* 226-251.

Louis, M. R. (1980b). Toward an understanding of career transitions. In C. B. Derr (Ed.), *Work, family, and the career* (pp. 200-218). New York: Praeger.

Marshall, C. (1985). Professional shock: The enculturation of the assistant principal. *Education and Urban Society, 18*(1), 28-58.

Mead, G. H. (1934). *Mind, self, and society.* Chicago: University of Chicago Press.

Megginson, D., & Clutterbuck, D. (1995). *Mentoring in action.* London: Kogan Page.

Merton, R. K. (1968). *Social theory and social structure.* New York: Free Press.

Meskin, J. (1974). The performance of women school administrators—A review of the literature. *Administrator's Notebook, 23*(1), 1-4.

Miller, J. (1988). Jobs and work. In N. Smelser (Ed.), *Handbook of sociology* (pp. 327-359). Newbury Park, CA: Sage.

Milstein, M. M. (1990). Rethinking the clinical aspects of preparation programs: From theory to practice. In S. L. Jacobson & J. A. Conway (Eds.), *Educational leadership in an age of reform* (pp. 119-130). New York: Longman.

Milstein, M. M., Bobroff, B. M., & Restine, L. N. (1991). *Internship programs in educational administration: A guide to preparing educational leaders.* New York: Teachers College Press.

Monteiro, T. (1977). Ethnicity and the perceptions of principals. *Integrated Education, 15*(3), 15-16.

Mortimer, J. T., & Simmons, R. G. (1978). Adult socialization. *Annual Review of Sociology, 4*, 421-454.

Muse, I. D., Wasden, F. D., & Thomas, G. J. (1988). *The mentor principal: Handbook.* Provo, UT: Brigham Young University.

Nash, D., & Treffinger, D. (1993). *The mentor: A step-by-step guide to creating an effective mentor program in your school.* Waco, TX: Prufrock.

Nelson, R. (1986). *The organizational socialization of public school administrators.* Unpublished doctoral dissertation, University of Oregon, Eugene.

Nicholson, N. (1984). A theory of work role transitions. *Administrative Science Quarterly, 29*(2), 172-191.

Nicholson, N. (1987). The transition cycle: A conceptual framework for the analysis of change and human resources management. In K. M. Rowland & G. R. Ferris (Eds.), *Research in personnel and human resources management* (Vol. 5, pp. 167-222). Greenwich, CT: JAI.

Nicholson, N., & West, M. (1989). Transitions, work histories, and careers. In M. B. Arthur, D. T. Hall, & B. S. Lawrence (Eds.), *Handbook of career theory* (pp. 181-201). New York: Cambridge University Press.

O'Brien, D. E. (1988). Taking the role of principal: A qualitative investigation of socialization during the first year (Doctoral dissertation, Kent State University, 1988). *Dissertation Abstracts International, 50*, 1513-A.

Odden, A. R. (1995). *Educational leadership for America's schools.* New York: McGraw-Hill.

Odell, S. J. (1989). Developing support programs for beginning teachers. In R. A. Edelfelt (Ed.), *Beginning teacher assistance programs.* Reston, VA: Association of Teacher Educators.

Odell, S. J. (1990). Support of new teachers. In T. M. Bey & C. T. Holmes (Eds.), *Mentoring: Developing successful new teachers* (pp. 3-23). Reston, VA: Association of Teacher Educators.

Ondrack, D. A. (1975). Socialization in professional schools. *Administrative Science Quarterly, 20,* 97-103.

Ortiz, F. I. (1982). *Career patterns in education: Women, men and minorities in public school administration.* New York: Praeger.

Ortiz, F. I., & Marshall, C. (1988). Women in educational administration. In N. J. Boyan (Ed.), *Handbook of research on educational administration* (pp. 123-144). New York: Longman.

Parkay, F. W. (1988). Reflections of a protégé. *Theory Into Practice, 27*(3), 195-200.

Parkay, F. W., Currie, G. D., & Rhodes, J. W. (1992). Professional socialization: A longitudinal study of first-time high school principals. *Educational Administration Quarterly, 28*(1), 43-75.

Pascale, R. (1984, May 28). Fitting new employees into the company culture. *Fortune,* pp. 28-43.

Peterson, K. D. (1977-1978). The principal's tasks. *Administrator's Notebook, 26,* 1-4.

Peterson, K. D. (1984). Mechanisms of administrative control over managers in educational organizations. *Administrative Science Quarterly, 29,* 573-597.

Peterson, K. D. (1986). Principals' work, socialization, and training: Developing more effective leaders. *Theory Into Practice, 25*(3), 151-155.

Peterson, K. D. (1987). An organizational perspective on career movement. *Administrator's Notebook, 32*(2), 1-4.

Phillips-Jones, L. (1982). *Mentors and protégés.* New York: Arbor House.

Post, D. (1992). Through Joshua Gap: Curricular control and the constructed community. *Teacher's College Press, 93*(4), 673-696.

Reed, D. B., & Himmler, A. H. (1985). The work of the secondary assistant principalship: A field study. *Education and Urban Society, 18*(1), 59-84.

Roche, G. R. (1979). Much ado about mentors. *Harvard Business Review, 57*(1), 14-16, 20, 24-27.

Ronkowski, S., & Iannaccone, L. (1989, March). *Socialization research in administration, graduate school, and other professions.* Paper presented at the annual meeting of the American Educational Research Association, San Francisco.

Schein, E. H. (1964). How to break in the college graduate. *Harvard Business Review, 42,* 68-76.

Schein, E. H. (1971a). The individual, the organization, and the career: A conceptual scheme. *Journal of Applied Behavioral Science, 7,* 401-426.

Schein, E. H. (1971b). Occupational socialization in the professions: The case of the role innovator. *Journal of Psychiatric Research, 8,* 521-530.

Schein, E. H. (1978). *Career dynamics: Matching individual and organizational needs.* Reading, MA: Addison-Wesley.

Schein, E. H. (1988, Fall). Organizational socialization and the profession of management. *Sloan Management Review,* pp. 53-65. (Reprinted from *Industrial Management Review,* 1968, *9,* 1-16)

Schein, E. H. (1992). *Organizational culture and leadership* (2nd ed.). San Francisco: Jossey-Bass.

Schein, E. H., & Ott, J. S. (1962). The legitimacy of organizational influence. *American Journal of Sociology, 67,* 682-689.

Schools and staffing survey—1993-1994 (public school administrators questionnaire) [Machine-readable data file]. (1993). Washington, DC: National Center for Educational Statistics, Office of Educational Research and Improvement, U.S. Department of Education.

Sergiovanni, T. (1992). *Moral leadership: Getting to the heart of school reform.* San Francisco: Jossey-Bass.

Shackelford, J. A. (1992). An uphill battle: Socialization of a novice female elementary principal (Doctoral dissertation, Oklahoma State University, 1992). *Dissertation Abstracts International, 54,* 767-A.

Shakeshaft, C. (1987). *Women in educational administration.* Newbury Park, CA: Sage.

Shakeshaft, C., & Hanson, M. (1986). Androcentric bias in the Educational Administration Quarterly. *Educational Administration Quarterly, 22*(1), 68-92.

Spady, W. G. (1985). The vice-principal as an agent of instructional reform. *Education and Urban Society, 18*(1), 107-120.

Speck, M., & Krovetz, M. (1996). Developing effective peer coaching experiences for school administrators. *ERS Spectrum: Journal of School Research and Information, 14*(1), 37-42.

Sperry, D. J., & Crow, G. M. (1996). Demographic characteristics of Utah school administrators. In P. Galvin & D. Sperry (Eds.), *Conditions of educational leadership in Utah, 1995-96 yearbook of the Educational Policy Center* (pp. 7-33). Salt Lake City: University of Utah, Educational Policy Center.

Stonehocker, C. L. (1992). *Protégé organizational socialization: Uncertainty reduction as a function of involvement in a mentoring relation-*

ship. Unpublished master's thesis, San Diego State University, San Diego, CA.

Sweeney, J., Licklider, B. L., Joekel, R. G., Wendel, F. C., Murray, R., Van Horn, D., Smith, E., & Turner, T. (1993). Problem analysis. In S. D. Thompson (Ed.), *Principals for our changing schools: Knowledge and skill base* (pp. 3-1 to 3-25). Fairfax, VA: National Policy Board for Educational Administration.

Teddlie, C., & Stringfield, S. (1993). *Schools make a difference: Lessons learned from a 10-year study of school effects.* New York: Teachers College Press.

Tomlinson, P. (1995). *Understanding mentoring: Reflective strategies for school-based teacher preparation.* Buckingham, UK: Open University Press.

Torrance, E. P. (1984). *Mentor relationships: How they aid creative achievement, endure, change, and die.* Buffalo, NY: Bearly.

Trice, H. M. (1993). *Occupational subcultures in the workplace.* Ithaca, NY: ILR Press.

Turner, V. W. (1970). Betwixt and between: The liminal period in rites of passage. In E. A. Hammel & W. S. Simons (Eds.), *Man makes sense* (pp. 354-369). Boston: Little, Brown.

Turoczy, A. T. (1996, October). *The road to school administration: Experiences of hopefuls in a preparation program.* Paper presented at the Fall conference of the University Council for Educational Administration, Louisville, KY.

Van Gennep, A. (1960) . *The rites of passage* (M. B. Vizedom & G. L. Caffee, Trans.). Chicago: University of Chicago Press. (Original work published in 1909)

Van Maanen, J. (1976). Breaking in: Socialization to work. In R. Dubin (Ed.), *Handbook of work, organization and society* (pp. 67-130). Chicago: Rand McNally.

Van Maanen, J. (1984). Doing new things in old ways: The chains of socialization. In J. L. Bess (Ed.), *College and university organization* (pp. 211-247). New York: New York University Press.

Van Maanen, J., & Barley, S. R. (1984). Occupational communities: Culture and control in organizations. *Research in Organizational Behavior, 6,* 287-365.

Van Maanen, J., & Schein, E. H. (1979). Toward a theory of organizational socialization. In L. Cummings & B. Staw (Eds.), *Research in organizational behavior* (pp. 209-264). Greenwich, CT: JAI.

Walker, A., & Stott, K. (1993). Preparing for leadership in schools: The mentoring contribution. In B. J. Caldwell & E. M. A. Carter (Eds.), *The return of the mentor: Strategies for workplace learning* (pp. 77-90). London: Falmer.

Weick, K. E. (1979). *The social psychology of organizing* (2nd ed.). Reading, MA: Addison-Wesley.

Weindling, D. (1992). New heads for old: Beginning principals in the United Kingdom. In F. W. Parkay & G. E. Hall (Eds.), *Becoming a principal: The challenges of beginning leadership* (pp. 329-348). Needham Heights, MA: Allyn & Bacon.

Weindling, D., & Earley, P. (1987). *Secondary headship: The first years.* Philadelphia: NFER-Nelson.

Wentworth, W. M. (1980). *Context and understanding: An inquiry into socialization theory.* New York: Elsevier.

Wheeler, S. (1966). The structure of formally organized socialization settings. In O. Brim & S. Wheeler (Eds.), *Socialization after childhood: Two essays* (pp. 51-105). New York: John Wiley.

Wilson, C. E. (1986). *The influence of communication network involvement on socialization in organizations.* Unpublished doctoral dissertation, University of Washington, Seattle.

Zey, M. G. (1984). *The mentor connection.* Homewood, IL: Dow Jones-Irwin.

Index

**CORWIN
PRESS**

The Corwin Press logo—a raven striding across an open book—represents the happy union of courage and learning. We are a professional-level publisher of books and journals for K–12 educators, and we are committed to creating and providing resources that embody these qualities. Corwin's motto is "Success for All Learners."